TEN CITIES
TEN POETS
CITIES

Other Recent Work Anthologies:
Seam: Prose Poems
Pulse: Prose Poems
The Taoist Elements
5 6 7 8

TEN CITIES
TEN POETS
CITIES

edited by
Paul Hetherington and
Shane Strange

RECENT
WORK
PRESS

Cities: Ten Poets, Ten Cities
Recent Work Press
Canberra, Australia

Copyright © the authors, 2017

National Library of Australia
Cataloguing-in-Publication entry.

Cities: Ten Poets, Ten Cities
edited by Paul Hetherington and Shane Strange

ISBN: 9780995353862 (paperback)

Australian poetry
Poetry—21st century

All rights reserved. This book is copyright. Except for private study, research, criticism or reviews as permitted under the Copyright Act, no part of this book may be reproduced stored in a retrieval system, or transmitted in any form by any means without prior written permission. Enquiries should be addressed to the publisher.

Cover illustration: 1266 by Sergey Norin, reproduced under Creative Commons 2.0 licence.

Cover design: Recent Work Press
Set in Bembo 11pt

recentworkpress.com

CONTENTS

NO SINGLE CITY   1
Paul Hetherington and Shane Strange

SYDNEY   1
Ross Gibson

KYOTO   15
Shane Strange

SINGAPORE   29
Alvin Pang

MUMBAI   43
Pooja Nansi

MOSCOW   55
Subhash Jaireth

HAIFA   69
Niloofar Fanaiyan

CAPE TOWN   81
Jen Webb

ROME   95
Paul Hetherington

NEW ORLEANS   109
Cassandra Atherton

ANONYMOUS   123
Paul Munden

NO SINGLE CITY

1. The fragmented and blind

No city is any one thing, and no city is able to be fully known or seen. Large cities are variously fragmented, including in the ways in which people experience or perceive them. The inhabitants of these cities know the districts where they live, work, travel and shop rather than having a detailed sense of the whole. Daniel Kozak writes that 'it can be argued that within postmodernism the starting point is recognition and celebration of a "fragmentary living" in contemporary metropolises' (2008: 241). Michel de Certeau writes of the blindness of a city's inhabitants, who do not have access to a 'celestial eye' able to comprehend a city in its entirety:

> The ordinary practitioners of the city live 'down below,' below the thresholds at which visibility begins. They walk—an elementary form of this experience of the city ... The paths that correspond in this intertwining, unrecognized poems in which each body is an element signed by many others, elude legibility. It is as though the practices organizing a bustling city were characterized by their blindness. (1984: 93)

Partly as a result of fragmentation and this sense of blindness, poets—as they construe cities in language—often make imagery that speaks of the strangeness and particularity of city life. They rarely seek to represent cities in their entirety; rather, they know parts of cities; specific places and certain kinds of interactions within cities, ways to travel through and about and around cities. The city as a whole remains an abstraction.

Poets have been responding in such ways for as long as cities have existed and poems have been made. Burton Pike writes that:

> Since there has been literature, there have been cities in literature. We unthinkingly consider this phenomenon modern, but it goes back

to the early epic and mythic thought. We cannot imagine *Gilgamesh*, the Bible, the *Iliad*, or the *Aeneid*, without their cities. (1981: 3)

The English Romantic poets featured cities in important works—William Blake's 'London' and William Wordsworth's *The Prelude* are examples of poems that excoriate the rise of cities in 19th-century life. Here is Wordsworth on the subject:

> Oh, blank confusion! true epitome
> Of what the mighty City is herself,
> To thousands upon thousands of her sons,
> Living amid the same perpetual whirl
> Of trivial objects, melted and reduced
> To one identity, by differences
> That have no law, no meaning, and no end— (1995: 291-92)

In the 19th and 20th centuries American poets also wrote in spellbinding ways about city life. As Walt Whitman mapped a mid-nineteenth century ferry journey between Brooklyn and Manhattan, he articulated an almost euphoric idea of the city as the embodiment of democratic and transcendentalist values. This is the poem 'Crossing Brooklyn Ferry', in which he celebrates 'The simple, compact, well-join'd scheme, myself disintegrated, everyone disintegrated yet part of the scheme,/ The similitudes of the past and those of the future,/ The glories strung like beads on my smallest sights and hearings, on the walk in the street and the passage over the river' (1973: 160). For Whitman in this poem the city embodies fecundity and promise. It is a metaphor for being fully alive.

Yet an ambivalent note is sounded. Whitman remains uncertain about whether the city he evokes actually possesses the values he espouses. He asks Brooklyn and Manhattan to 'bring your freight, bring your shows, ample and sufficient rivers,/ Expand, being than which none else is perhaps more spiritual,/ Keep your places, objects than which none else is more lasting'. The equivocal phrase 'perhaps more spiritual' is telling here and Pike has observed that in such lines Whitman 'is not expressing values he shares with his beloved fellow-citizens, but values he wants them to have' (1981: 85).

Whitman maintained a deliberately old-fashioned vision in his final version of the poem even as it claimed to present a vision of a vibrant future. It foregrounds the to-and-fro of disconnected parts of a city in the throes of being built rather than a more homogenous and better connected whole, and it is the latent potential of the city suggested by its variousness and the separateness of its parts that appeals to the poet. Whitman could not have written 'Crossing Brooklyn Ferry' 50 years later when New York City had developed in ways that were very different from the future he had imagined.

Whitman's optimistic vision did not prove to be sustainable in the 20th century, however powerful his poem remains. By the time T.S. Eliot wrote 'Preludes' in 1917, the city—in this case London—was characterised, with a decidedly post-Romantic emphasis, as possessing stretched souls and 'broken blinds and chimney-pots' (1954: 22). Eliot completed 'The Waste Land' a few years later by which time he had further transformed his vision of London into an 'Unreal city,/ Under the brown fog of a winter dawn' (1954: 53).

New York was also re-envisioned in the 20th century. One of the most celebrated and self-consciously poetic visitors to New York was Federico Garcia Lorca, who arrived in 1929 just prior to the stock market crash that ushered in the Great Depression. The meeting in Lorca of personal and public despair produced poetry of a savage and sometimes surreal disjuncture. This is a poetry in which imagery often floats away from clear meaning, or in which meaning is clear but the imagery is mixed; which moves almost arbitrarily between denotation and connotation; and in which large abstractions are thrown out almost casually: 'Dawn in New York has/ four columns of mire/ and a hurricane of black pigeons/ splashing in the putrid waters…' (2008: 73).

Hazel Smith (2000: 58) discusses the way in which the poems of mid-20th century New Yorker Frank O'Hara 'vary in the degree to which they dislocate the city' and quotes the opening of O'Hara's well-known poem memorialising the singer Billie Holiday:

It is 12:20 in New York a Friday
three days after Bastille day, yes

> it is 1959 and I go get a shoeshine
> because I will get off the 4:19 in Easthampton
> at 7:15 and then go straight to dinner
> and I don't know the people who will feed me (O'Hara 1979: 325)

As we have written elsewhere, this poem's conceit 'is that it follows a journey on foot that O'Hara makes through New York. It is a journey that celebrates the quotidian at the same time as it claims a special significance for the day in which it is set' (Strange and Hetherington 2014: 6).

2. Poetry and the postmodern city

In later 20th- and early 21st-century poetry, images of cities begin to stand metonymically for, and bleed into, the very idea of postmodernity until the two concepts are hardly distinct or separate. For instance, in Stephen Spender's 20th-century vision of a failing civilisation ('the failure of banks/ The failure of cathedrals and the declared insanity of our rulers'), the image of the brilliant city is at the nub of crisis:

> After they have tired of the brilliance of cities
> And of striving for office where at last they may languish
> Hung round with easy chains until
> Death and Jerusalem glorify also the crossing-sweeper:
> Then those streets the rich built and their easy love
> Fade like old cloths, and it is death stalks through life
> Grinning white through all faces
> Clean and equal like the shine from snow. (1965: 256)

This is poetry that despairs of modernity (or, at least, of modern capitalism) and in which the city symbolises what is contemporary, frail and false.

Western Australian poet Dennis Haskell conjures another contemporary vision of the city and globalisation:

> In the corridors of plush hotels
> blank, windowless walls. A deep silence dwells
>
> in front of every slab plain door,
> knowing this its market. Along the floor
>
> lush carpet depicts footsteps
> that no eye ever sees. The precepts
>
> of payment demand singularity
> of being, although sameness must be
>
> the outcome. (2006: 52-53)

This is a depiction of a kind of death-in-life; of a bland, technocratic, citified and stultified existence that is also a willed separation from the city's more vigorous life, including, as he says later in the poem, elbows that 'bump on city streets' (2006: 53). It is an example of the way in which the 'made' nature of city environments often preoccupies contemporary poets.

Cities are also canyoned with the space that surrounds skyscrapers and other buildings. Such space may be read as enshrining what is unknowable or barely knowable—human disconnection from, but close proximity to the unknowable and the wild; human society as a sprawling and ramifying series of (actual and linguistic) disjunctures; and the inscription of absence among assertive presence. The New York poet Charles North writes in the first part of 'The Postcard Element in Winter':

> Supposing the wildlife became a person
> who suddenly sprouted into an infinite number of ideas
> each idea casting an ideal glow from canyon to canyon
> like the most wandering star space
> whose atmosphere singes the very park—
> as though the city existed to be barreled through
> in spite of the windy quiet on its face
> the factory snap, the raw potatoes and practicing the bassoon
> (1999: 104)

This is not so much a vision of a city, as a vision of unstable transformations inhabiting an equally unstable sense of a place. The city itself barely exists in this poem except as something to be 'barreled through'. It is a few disconnected remnants; and tacked on poetic gestures. How may such a city (even obscurely) be understood? Such questions were given added weight and poignancy after the September 11 2001 attacks on the World Trade Center complex. The poet Deborah Garrison begins a poem about these events with the lines: 'I saw you walking through Newark Penn Station/ in your shoes of white ash' (Lundberg 2011: n.pag.).

3. Reclaiming the city

Despite the sometimes bewildering and hostile faces of cities, many of us inhabit them. They surround and shape us, fashioning many of our large and small assumptions and attitudes. Notwithstanding their size, we often believe that we know them intimately, or at least with a special sense of familiarity. Further, there is sometimes a sense that the poet speaks with a consciousness of the city; a consciousness that is born out of and remains intrinsic to a place. Delmore Schwartz in 'America, America!' provides one such post-Whitmanesque vision of the city, celebrating the way the city 'looks' as we look; understanding that our vision of the city is also the city's vision of us:

> — This is the city self, looking from window to lighted window
> When the squares and checks of faintly yellow light
> Shine at night, upon a huge dim board and slab-like tombs,
> Hiding many lives. It is the city consciousness
> Which sees and says: more: more and more: always more.
> (Schwartz 1989: 4)

Schwartz's idea of the modern city encompasses 'the secret city in the heart and mind' and 'the song of the natural city self' (1989: 4), emphasising the role of individuals in making their own understanding of their cities. It speaks of, and to, the multiplicities of the city, and of how fragmentation and an evolving profusion of city experience can be part of what the modern city-dweller understands, and even welcomes and embraces.

In this way, although cities remain complex and unknowable in any absolute sense, they are also often familiar and even unsurprising. Part of the pleasure of city living is that a city may be experienced in endlessly changing ways—more ways than can be enumerated—as if cities demand of their inhabitants the cultivation of protean and shifting selves and shapes. Cities may be approached from the standpoints of workers, wanderers, tourists, students, lovers and flâneurs—and from many other standpoints, too. They may be seen from below, above, from level ground, and from slanted perspectives. They may be passed through, inhabited for a lifetime, glimpsed from a distance, nostalgically remembered, loved, liked, hated, wept over and gloried in.

We may feel that we know a city intimately, or merely have a sense of its mysteries through fleeting perceptions. We may characterise a particular city in broad gestures, or may represent our experiences of a city as personal, highly specific and not easily subject to broad characterisation. We may do all of this at once, taking pleasure in the contradictions of trying to understand what a city may be. Cities ask us to invent not only ourselves, but a view of ourselves within the cityscapes we imagine.

As poets construct new perspectives on cities, they are able to reclaim spaces that might otherwise seem too large, or too fragmented and problematic for sustained consideration. They are in some respects like literary psychogeographers who 'navigate [a city's] physical terrain as mental terrain too' (Mitchell et al 2009: n.pag.). Poetry is an important way of undertaking such reclamation; of bringing into our own imaginary the city as we understand it, however incompletely and however provisionally. Cities may sometimes appear mysterious and even paradoxical, but poetry has the capacity to speak articulately of such paradox and mystery.

In any case, sometimes a city's mysteries are not so far from home and may be revealed in and through the mundane and the quotidian. Often we gather a sense of a city by shopping in it or drinking and eating at its cafes, bars and restaurants; by walking its streets or by exchanging small talk with its people. And, not infrequently, one city will remind us of other cities, so that our experiences in one place will be ghosted by experiences in other locations.

Such multiple perspectives remind us how human beings intersect in complex and strange ways, perhaps especially in postcolonial contexts where so many hauntings are connected to problematic histories of place, invasion and settlement. Whatever their histories may be, places often become emblematic of certain kinds of thinking, doing and connecting with others. If cities are ghosted, and sometimes ghostly in our apprehension, these ghosts inhabit cities' landscapes, histories, people, and the very sounds and smells of the street.

We are able to speak back to the hubbub of cities. We are able to make poems that create a legibility for the cities we inhabit. Such practices are a counter to the blindness of city living; and they are a way of mapping our inscriptions of a city onto its bustling life. Despite the abstract nature of cities, poets are frequently able to distil, define and name important aspects of city life, employing imagery and figurative language to animate their visions of cities and to transform and gesture at—or symbolise or encapsulate—the brick and concrete and rubble of cities; their thoroughfares and byways; their buildings and abandoned ground. As poets speak for themselves in the city, so they hear the city's ruminations inflecting their work. This is part of what it means to write about cities—it is to listen to and inscribe the rhythms and meanings that the city is always making.

Every city 'speaks' differently to every one of its inhabitants and each poem about cities is part of an individual's dialogue with a city, characterised by particular inflections and frequently addressing their lived experiences, however obliquely. As poets make cities their own, readers are able to travel with them to the particularities of time, place and space that they conjure. Every poem about a city is a facet of that city as someone has seen and imagined it; as it has been construed, interpreted, captured, configured and mapped.

4. This anthology

In formulating this anthology, we were inspired by our visits to two of the world's ancient and venerated cities, Rome and Kyoto—historical capitals of their respective worlds. Both of us also have a longstanding interest in the way cities and writing about cities have evolved and continue to evolve. We wondered about other cities, and the ways in which poet-colleagues might construe them in poetry. We asked some of the poets represented in this volume to write about specific cities—knowing of their interest in those places—and in other cases we left the choice of the city to the poet, wanting to discover what place whetted their poetic appetite.

The collection that has resulted shows the 'glamour' of certain cities, particularly Sydney and New Orleans; and emphasises what one may call the contemporary-historical appeal of Rome and Kyoto. The cities of Cape Town and Singapore have a central significance in, respectively, Jen Webb's and Alvin Pang's personal lives and memories; and other cities are enmeshed in various poets' individual romantic, familial or religious experiences (Mumbai, Moscow and Haifa). Overall, we have a group of cities represented in this volume that are as distinctive as the poetic voices that conjure them. They are all familiar and mysterious, in different ways—and this last quality is further foregrounded by Paul Munden's poems about notional and anonymous cities.

There is evidence in this volume of the way place and memory are frequently admixed, and how lived experience is filtered and condensed into telling forms of utterance through the creative writing process. All the poets included have revealed something about their city through their styles as well as through their works' content. Ross Gibson is well known for writing about the dark heart of Sydney, and here we find him pursuing these preoccupations again, revealing a city whose appeal is shadowed by its failings, even as he acknowledges that these shadows are part of what makes the city something of an obsession for him ('A geist that puts hooks in where you do your hardest wanting').

In exploring 'New Orleans', Cassandra Atherton adopts a deft intertextual mode, conjuring literary allusions and connections to places and landmarks in this famous city while exploring how her personal knowledge of and encounters with New Orleans further enliven, complicate and inflect her sense of the city. Her writing moves and eddies through time and space, doubly anchored in her cultural knowledge and New Orleans' particularities. Alvin Pang articulates a deeply intimate understanding of 'Singapore', exploring a variety of highly evocative and sometimes ambiguous tropes, trying—as he says in the notes to this volume—to express the city's 'plural, intersecting histories, both personal and public'. The movement of this poetic rendering of Singapore is complex, embedded in multivalent perspectives and disorientating juxtapositions, much like the city itself.

In Jen Webb's 'Cape Town' the grandeur of the natural landscape frames some of the difficult histories of that place, which is also expressed in terms of personal subjectivities and a deeply embedded sense of how provisional many of our acts and decisions are ('You climbed the breakwater, measuring against the sea our public shame.') In these poems, Cape Town remains a city steeped in uncertainty and crisis, and a site of many puzzles and questions. Subhash Jaireth's 'Moscow' is a richly observed and deeply layered vision of a city dressed in everyday beauty and resonant stories. This is certainly not the grim, uniform misery that one might otherwise conjure when reflecting on the Soviet Union in the mid-1970s. We find in Jaireth's work a deep affection for a sometimes opaque place.

Pooja Nansi takes the reader into a personal history of her family in 'Mumbai'. In her work the fragmentations and dislocations associated with modern metropolises aligns with a fractured family history and attenuated memories as she draws us towards specific locales. She conjures condensed, poetic narratives focused on a questing longing and a keen sense of human strangeness. Niloofar Fanaiyan's 'Haifa' evokes a city which she returns to regularly and which draws people from around the world as a religious centre, while maintaining its own idiosyncratic particularities, including customs and curiosities that she observes keenly. Her affection for the city is written closely and rhythmically into her work.

Paul Hetherington's poems are often closely focused, their prose poetical stanzas more like rooms than the plazas, cathedrals or ruins of 'Rome'. They express intimations and fragments of city living through ruminations about death and human relationships, suggesting how the small is able to overwrite the large where human subjectivity is concerned. In 'Kyoto', Shane Strange understands the city from the viewpoint of a visitor who has connected powerfully with its elaborately-made 'thousand-year' identity. His nuanced works straddle the divide between knowing and not-knowing a place; cognisant of its fascinations, tantalisations and new provocations, and paying homage to a grounded encounter between the poetic imagination and an exquisitely layered urban culture.

And Paul Munden's perpendicular take on the city offers a release from quotidian reality in conjuring 'anonymous' cities that are never quite what we know. Yet the actual haunts his work, overlapping with what he invents, reminding us that cities are as much a place of the mind as places made of buildings, roads and malls. If these poems are cities of the imagination, they are also (and yet not quite) cities we too have imagined or encountered.

Readers will notice that all of the works in this volume are prose poems. We asked a number of people familiar to us through the International Poetry Studies Institute's Prose Poetry Project to participate in this anthology, and other participants seemed to divine that this was the required form. To help orient (or dis-orient) the reader we asked the poets to furnish their sequences with a timeframe. And, finally, please note that the cities have been arranged geographically by distance from the prime meridian or, more precisely, from the most easterly latitude to the most westerly. In doing so, we aimed to see these poems set off in Sydney, Australia and follow the sun's journey across the globe.

-Paul Hetherington and Shane Strange

Works cited

De Certeau, Michel 1984 *The Practice of Everyday Life* (transl by Steven F Rendall), Berkeley: University of California Press

Eliot TS 1954 *Selected Poems*, London: Faber and Faber

Haskell, Dennis 2006 *All the Time in the World*, Cambridge: Salt

Kozak, Daniel 2008 'Assessing Urban Fragmentation: The emergence of new typologies in central Buenos Aires', in Mike Jenks, Daniel Kozak and Pattaranan Takkanon (eds), *World Cities and Urban Form: Fragmented, polycentric, sustainable?*, London and New York: Routledge, 239-258

Lorca, Frederico Garcia 2008 *Poet in New York: A bilingual edition*, transl Pablo Medina and Mark Statman, New York: Grove

Lundberg, John 2011 'Remembering 9/11 Through Poetry', The Huffington Post, 17 November 2011, http://www.huffingtonpost.com/john-lundberg/remembering-911-through-p_b_712416.html (accessed 4 April 2017)

Mitchell, Natasha, Stephen Burstow, Elizabeth Farrelly, Merlin Coverly, Elaena Gardener 2009 'Psychogeography: Discovering the mental terrain of the city', transcript of ABC radio program All in the Mind, 5 September 2009, http://www.abc.net.au/radionational/programs/allinthemind/psychogeography-discovering-the-mental-terrain-of/3062988#transcript (accessed 4 April 2017)

O'Hara, Frank 1979 *The Collected Poems of Frank O'Hara*, ed Donald Allen, New York: Knopf

Pike, Burton 1981 *The Image of the City in Modern Literature*, Princeton: Princeton University Press

Schwartz, Delmore 1989 *Last and Lost Poems*, rev ed, ed Robert Phillips, New York: New Directions

Spender, Stephen 1965 'After They Have Tired' in *The Faber Book of Modern Verse*, ed. Michael Roberts, rev Donald Hall, London: Faber, 256-57

Smith, Hazel 2000 *Hyperscapes in the Poetry of Frank O'Hara: Difference/homosexuality/topography*, Liverpool: Liverpool University Press

Strange, S and P Hetherington 2014, 'Making the city otherwise: Ways of teaching the writing of poetry', in *The Minding the Gap: Writing Across thresholds and fault lines papers*—The Refereed Proceedings of the 19th conference of the Australasian Association of Writing Programs, 2014, ed Gail Pittaway, Alex Lodge and Lisa Smithies, ISBN 9780980757385, https://d3n8a8pro7vhmx.cloudfront.net/theaawp/pages/156/attachments/original/1426481408/Strange__Hetherington_MakingCityOtherwise.pdf?1426481408 (accessed 30 March 2015)

Whitman, Walt 1973 *Leaves of Grass,* ed Sculley Bradley and Harold W Blodgett, New York: WW Norton

Wordsworth, William 1995 *The Prelude: The four texts* (1798, 1799, 1805, 1850), ed Jonathan Wordsworth, London: Penguin

SYDNEY

sometime last week

ROSS GIBSON

UTC+11 • 33°52'S / 151°12'E

1

It's aqueous. Shiny. Shifty. Stupid and braggart. Gorgeous beyond measure. Cruel and exorbitant. A geist that puts hooks in where you do your hardest wanting.

2

The biggest fools come from elsewhere. They fall in love with the place before they know much about it, falling hard, beyond reason, beyond hope of recovery. (I know because I fell that way.) Careless about decrepitude, the fist of corruption.

The fist of corruption?

Witness the:

>Land Grabbing.
>
>Coal Mining.
>
>Booze Licensing.
>
>Taxes on Gambling.

Those four digits wrap around the town, counter-clasped by a stub-thumbed

>Police Force.

Throttling the town since 1788.

Never once letting go.

3

Lovelorn saps might try to get the hell out of town.

They might even succeed, scattering north, south, east or west.

But remember, these renegades have been whipped by their first love. So if they happen to backslide—say they return on a day when the town vamps a few come-hither guises and utters sparkling wattle nectar—then every pledge and resolve will just go to mist.

4

Sandstone ridge country. Outer northwestern suburbs.

Footsteps go frantic across terracotta roof-tiles while, downstairs in the lamplight, two faces twitch close-up before vision shifts wide to a car-crash that's tiny-distant to look at but massive on the soundtrack.

Fade to quiet black.

Cut hard to a dark kitchen where blunt objects plummet at the camera before a door careens open and flames start to surge along a green curtain.

Meanwhile, back at the car-crash, the screech of a fruitbat brings lightning to a bent man. He's struggling while standing with loose space all around him. Now his mannerisms are your mannerisms and time blows like a starburst and hangs in soft air.

5

Falling into chloroform, all images gather and cloud-structures crumble without sound, except for mercenary winds. Which unfairly howl. Still a star persists dozing inside its dank cavern long after midnight has stopped stunning the air.

The ground below is called Five Dock, where colour sleeps in dark lungs of water while a sick whale bumps and re-bumps an ammoniac pontoon. Downwind, a lonely thunderclap stirs fog overrunning a taut vapid shire.

Spend six hours of mumbling. Beckon dazed sunlight. Tremble, stumble, brace and breathe slowly.

6

Servile foliage kicks and tosses in stormy insurrection. Twitched lines of lightning patrol the templed skies. Drumthunder. Silence. Angophora whispers seditious quips about the sun. Flocking corellas hang like a rosary. Drapes jerk. A door slams. A cockatoo flees, screaming, to the lee-side of a bruised cloud.

7

At the art Biennale on Cockatoo Island, scrummed images are gathered by a scrapcatcher magnet lolling off a rusty crane and seagulls boggle above tensioned thick nylon lines strung trapezoid in a pest-deterrent scheme scaled out to the west shoreline. Utilitarian, yes—this gullenspooker—but it's the best art on show maybe. ('Everybody says that,' deadpans the dude in the Info Van.)

Colour clamours here and there, save in the graphite zones and in soundscapes booming foghorn-style. And then you find Bill Forsyth's pendular field which just GOES like this:

> making and remaking
>
> long furrows of perspective
>
> to the eye
>
> and trajectories
>
> for the motive corps.

(Think: a flood that does not flow.)

When the ferry homebound comes back to the pier, you leave your best thoughts behind, also your feelings, crumpled and damp, trash on a mossy sandstone escalier.

8

skin salt sun skin salt sun skin salt head holding hat holding warmth holding head holding ardour slackening ardour slackening blood ardour hosing down blood cooling down blood hosing down cooling moonglow cooling moonglow flesh ripening flesh ripening salt sun skin night rainbow gleaming night rainbow gleaming night gleaming hotel yard snow dropper hotel yard snow dropper hotel yard nicotine ceiling nicotine sun skin flop house lothario salt flop gelid sky dawn bird call gelid sky bird dawn call sky heat hazed heat hazed sand stone wind flute sand stone wind sky dawn bird call gelid sky bird call flute dawn ogle windows ogle windows ogle lothario crime pattern capture crime pattern craving then indulging then craving then learning to walk again learning force flushing blossom force flushing less sleeping more swelling less sleeping more swelling scintilla water scintilla town lurk merchant town sandstone wind flute sand stone salt sun skin assault stone blood hose

9

aftermath smoulder aftermath wattle dust blood spatter smoulder sunrise nectar tang aftermath sunrise city silk filth spatter silk city thickening filth thickening fog horn pulse burgeoning fog dust 800 miles in 24 hours 800 hours in staggering trouble dazzle trouble strugglng trudging falling limping struggling looming staggering everywhere burgeon everywhere real estate bluster town booze betting smoky fuel estate real bluster dazzle trouble timetabled disordered tetanus wounds fuzzy forgetting ferry smoke skeining fog spatter forgetting disorder timetable storm struck sound track storm bluster town wound smoulder ejaculant spring trudging humid ejaculant dazzle larrikin tetanus skin spring wanting longing wanting sparkle yen gagging exhausted bubbling yen exhausted sparkle hubbub knee deep hubbub yen dazzle gagging humid spring tasting of rain smelling of sleep spring tasting smoky fuel hoax oyster fever hoax larrikin spatter black harbor water spritzing black nectar tang longing shimmer deep water shimmer humid bluster town

10

The street is suffused with a mood. Nat 'King' Cole sings a ballad.

Take clues from the house:

>A cake in the oven already cooling.

>A child's wooden wheeled rabbit.

>A fountain pen oozing.

Facts blunt and material. Examine them slowly.

Plain misadventure? Some signs mean just nothing. Carbon in residue. One man might be responsible. War wounded, no sweetheart. Tempted by expedience. Voice fuzzed with forbearance. Force meeting resistance. A life stored in grievance.

Everyone is surviving some kind of luck.

It's a town full of taverns that the locals call 'blood houses'. On lock-up at midnight men souse tiled bars with hoses. Red whorls in the water.

There's a force always working to warp any straight thing.

Hear that keening in the wind? No-one alive knows why it all started.

The worth of a man—in dollars & cents? What price for a girl's skin? Payment's in sweat. Sleep's overdue. How long does blood last? Can lightning do good? Is there harm in a colour?

Oil can ooze out of every square inch of skin.

Use a device with a switch for the adjustment of moods. Hear music from blown breath. Turn over a card.

Pulses all shifting. Excitement, then shame.

Shoes scrape on concrete.

Light shimmers a windscreen.
Curtail every plan now, contenting in memory, defining luck as a reservoir.

Step in a way no-one anticipates.

The sun might be a balm.

The steamed air a soft unguent.

KYOTO

December, 2015

SHANE STRANGE

UTC+9 • 35°01'N / 135°46'E

Osaka to Kyoto

Soviet architecture finds its analogue along this railway line. No petering out into suburbs and fields. No dialectic of country and town. Expressways tangle like roots in the air with unapologetic tower blocks: graveyards in the sky. Wires cut clouds into segments. Carriage windows fog in the cold. The mountains are green on the horizon, pegged down into earth by electricity pylons like fingers pressed into the nape of a neck.

Fushimi Inari Shrine

Cool stone lanterns, grey and mossy, held in valleys and along streams as fortuitous as a favour. The tinny pitch of thin bells worked by finger pulls on long ceremonial ribbons. Vermilion arches stretch into tunnels under crowded trees and the air tinged with a green you have never smelt before. On the way down grilled meats taste of salt and soy. Money changes hands. The fox, Kitsune, as refined as a brush stroke, watches on. After all, this is the shrine to which business men pray.

Kiyomizu-dera

leap   temple for the lovesick   Escher beams brace the platform high   leap   for broken legs steps cut into the mountain   through the winter forest clear water   falls up the mountain   incense smoke catches hair   this place of soft hatreds   purification   smell of fish broth and syrup   descend

Zen garden, Ryo-anji

Dark things keep his nose pushed into the ground. His face a scar in the earth: a shadow formed in gravel furrows. His eyes clean rocks breaking lines into circles. A small boy draws water from a fountain and his father holds a bamboo cup. A girl takes a photograph. The end of days.

Ceramics, Hosomi Museum

I.

A porcelain bowl on purple cloth. A milky blue eye at its base. A box to carry it in.

II.

The meiping vase shaped like a lover's hip (celadon in pale blue, inlaid with crane and cloud) draws the eye but forbids the hand.

Saisho-in

Follow the stone path to a graveyard cupped in the mountain cleft. The evening bell sounds dimly—slow beat of the mountain's heart. A pine tree grows in the grove. Cross a log bridge into the valley of the evening.

Kinka-kuji

A red machine—'English fortune'—100 yen to test the oracle.

A golden temple, razed by a monk, rebuilt in 1955.

Though autumn has passed, orange leaves on a maple.

Familiarity

His letters arrive in the morning post at the *machiya* house where you stay. You arrange to meet in Marayuma Park on New Year's Day, but don't keep the appointment. You glimpse him at a standing bar in Pontocho. You leave through a back alley, change accommodation, and change once more. You are in student digs in Ichijoji. You eat at the ramen houses, waiting in line like everyone else. You catch the train to Kurama to bathe at the onsen. On the walk from the station you see two violets growing on a tree and a butterfly drawn by the flowers. A hand grasps your shoulder.

Exchange value—Sanjusanjendo

The goddess of mercy has 33 hands, each representing 33 manifestations the goddess can take. The 33-armed goddess of mercy (perceiving the cries of the world) is replicated in Japanese cypress and gold leaf 1000 times. There are 33 spaces between the posts in this hall to house the 1000 statues, the 33,000 hands. There are 28 guardian deities protecting the goddess. A blessing costs 500 yen. A large prayer candle, 1000 yen. I buy a monkey statue and a box of incense.

Proprietor, Higashiyama

Peeling onions, her arms as taut as ropes. She wears rubber boots and denim jeans. She lights a cigarette, barks at the chef. There's something on TV. She watches for a while. My meal comes, and a beer. I eat and pay the bill. Her forehead is wide, her fine hair pulled back in a ponytail. A slight smudge of lipstick across her smoker's pucker.

A record of drifting ashore, Museum of Kyoto

The artist's notebook is filled with forms (watercolour over pencil) skewered on invisible sticks. Finely dressed women don't walk, they fold themselves forward. Soldiers hover on horses. A monkey with a parasol dances for benefit of garish faces. A bit of red among the blue.

Near Kyoto station

I carried my postcard to you in the rain and the words washed away and the post office was closed. As I passed the *Bar Populare* the waiter stood inside the door watching a line of empty barstools against the wall. A crowd caught me on the corner and washed me in to some place under fluorescent lighting and it yelled at me like a storm, and I remembered my eyes were sore, and people were staring at phones because it was the only way they knew home. When I got out of that place and found my way back, I had nothing, not the smallest thing, to show for it. And I thought about you, and how you kept me warm, and how sorry I was I hadn't written.

SINGAPORE

1972 ⟶ 2017

ALVIN PANG

UTC+8 • 1°17'N / 103°51'E

1.290270,103.851959 (2017)

'We had to make it look a bit more like Singapore—given it was Singapore'

not sporting lah, make people go extra drawsnakeaddleg mile to make the place look more like its own self. you see lah, all those years of speakgoodenglish until now people cannot tell this from manchester. got tall building, got peoplemountainpeoplesea shopping centre crowd, got rain, got grumpy taxi driver, got rush hour traffic, got scottish bridge, even got big grey building with fake greek columns, just like theirs! always like that: die die must sapu all their angus ross until they give up and cancel. cannot just be humble, know your place, pretend not to understand, smile. dog mouth cannot grow elephant teeth. asian road signs must be asian. asian buildings must be asian. asians must look asian, cannot be too clean or white or macam london banker. if not wait next time people confused cabut elsewhere, how? tax incentives wasted. tourism board angry. then finished. this kind of chapalang notthreenotfour island, who wants to come?

1.391381,103.981511 (1979-1983)

A British soldier walks out of Grandma's closet, walks down Netheravon Road towards Sealand, vanishing in the shadow of the sodium street-lamps. She tells us this before dinner, explaining why she wants to leave early. She is not distraught exactly: she's lived through the War after all; knows what these blooded beaches can account for; what a purple sky used to mean. But someone will have to take her home. Still, there is little point all of us decamping: the old chalet is paid up for the weekend and it is only Saturday. Flight can wait. Meanwhile, twilight. Chicken wings on the barbecue, Lee Kuan Yew on the radio, exhorting Asian values, hard work. Hard water comes out of the taps, this close to the sea, chalks our tea and salts it, makes it taste of old bones brewed too long in one of Grandma's double-boiled soups. She's almost forgotten she wants to leave now, watching her grandsons scamper across sandy grass with makeshift harpoons fletched from satay sticks and straw. Or did she leave at once, her lingering a wished-for, fashioned fancy? Years hence, Grandma long since gone, lovers end their lives in Chalet M. SARS prospects quarantine in the bungalows. Invisible hands trip a novelist, near the morgue of the old hospital (now hotel). She tells me this before dinner, with the same equanimity, the same grey in her fringe, her tongue-sharp Cantonese. Something about how memories groove. Our repetitions bleed through. Perhaps we scar time. We who live stories left behind, who try to forget fear. Marching without looking down or back.

1.328686,103.888349 (1982)

Each New Year you drive past the spot, all hope now. All value-add and mission and new paint. Now a gantried carpark, the blindside of the school field where you slumped, uniform torn and fauved with grass and mud because you read books. Or talked to girls. You're thinking how we place ourselves. Never learnt to speak bully but you knew when it was spoken. The gut blanch. The heart's blue chill. The wound alarm. Not daring to run, not when you were ten, nor now, but why stand up to it? Look at the flats here on Circuit Road, how they let themselves be stripped, their streaked facades rendered glaucous. Dredged from the bone up to suit the story. People try to live in them. What have you done with your surrender?

1.327932,103.886171 (1974-1984)

MacPherson. Some warheroed welltrod colonial secretary left his name to this estate become circuitous way to grow up not so much (fa/mo)thered as grand(pa/ma)ed, except on weekends and dinnertime often tardy, occasionally called off. When are they coming? An early surmise: time distends with wait. Dust in the common corridor apparates under the load of such attention. Cracks in the ashen pavement. Justcut shallots hitting the wok over the course of a decade. Then garlic, beancurd, friedfish, duskdescanting. Fluesong. Sandalwood. Tableau of neighbours. Palimpsest of routine. Every night this flat or that someone shouting and shouting back in their own tongue. Dictionary of cusses. Kitchenware drumset. TV volumes turned up, post-HongKongTVBdiscard, to HuangWenYong/XiangYun dialogue that ricochets between Blocks 40 and 41, as surrogate as stars can be to the leftbehind flock of the busyworking, huaren who don't jianghuayu enough, who need roots and trimmed branches and cunning husbandry. Mongrel3rd pulled to pedigree1st. Yes, better happened, but what isn't put down? The saidtoberich crone with the pinched eyes, who never threw out a thing, so her groundfloorunit festered into holdbreathwalkby sudor to be braved twice a day, toschool, fromschool. The samseng untuckedshirt prefects demanding choice cuts of the collectorcards (firstkings, winning rarities) for safe passage and no fear, only a kind of tollbooth caution, with weal enough for marbles and tuabehlong after class. Picked last but played. Voiddeck soccer. Corridor badminton. The monday garbagetruck grunge. The marketman whose appetite turned cancerous. His son who wanted to touchheretouchthere, smilestoppingly forward with nextdoorboy too young to refuse. The whiteloud funerals, their blue stripped tents, and sometimes the suona outjowled by dikir barat, the wedding crush waiting for the hearse to pass. Years it took to get back to the table, to sit with these first interminables. How to sound such undulations? How to deliver neat in the mouth a whisper of was that is still wanting? Ask. And ask again.

1.3276542,103.886443 (1978-1984)

On theywouldliketofuckwithoutbeinginterrupted weekdays he is at Grandma's on Circuit Road, translating childhood into willtheycomewilltheycome evenings, snout past the latched flaking 3-RoomFlat grilles, lugubrious, forsaking dinner. As if longing cancelled traffic, or desire. The maybedependsonhowlate phonecall, it wrecks the sunset. The tellhimtodohishomework lashes of rain, the black ink of them running, the curryandgravestone sour of dank on slab. This the era of songbirds along a common corridor, goodmorninguncle neighbours, persimmons, jasmine, pandan, bougainvillea in toosmall pots on makeshift balancedonbiscuittin shelves. The full stereo din of the monsoon shouting over the garlicsizzle over the scratchscratchscratch on jotter paper, stick figures heroic in a beautiful shooting war, showing up just in time.

1.341526,103.848966 (1981-1988)

Toa Payoh North. Beneath the manwomanlovinginprivate, the coy buakmedicine behind lockeddoor, the enemayelp, the carnage of tongues, a boy wondering what the pain is for. Home an earned treat. Home onceaweek love, and his own room, the latch jammed open, a rubber stopper to keep it from slamming in the 13thstorey wind. A carskid away, tarzanswinging across the stormdrain, the nameneverasked neighbour who could catch guppies with bare hands. The uncommon corridor where he seared a morsel of knee fooling around with a satay pit, how he learnt to start fires he could not stop. The sweet baconic porklite stench, the stalebutterontoast tang of Burnol selfsmeared and making things worse, shockshiver and a guiltful calm bandaging the sting, which must have been, given the charred coin falling away in piceous flakes, better to forget. Back when it used to flood, the white Lotus like in the Bond film floats past the stillthere Shell stop, not at all amphibious. He eavesdrops. He peeks at their Reflections ('77) on dubbed VHS. He helps with the mopfloor and the feedyourself. Across the street they've built a police station. His sister arrives shortly afterwards.

1.29457,103.838014 (1988-1990)

River Valley's river long since subdued, though once two labials on either side of the unscrubbed stream, birthcanal of all this spending, all dressed to be discordant but unpractised in jazz. A merchant, two wives, three units on a single unkempt floor, the discollected, obstreperous brood. Not clannish, exactly, but a clan. Laying claim by blood to a thicker materiality. The patriarch made provisions (foresight!) for both manorwings (fairness!), enjoined consensus with distributed votekeys (wisdom!) but forgot forgetting (dementia!) and basic human shortfall so the feud funded a decade of muchobliged lawyering, tothisday continues, like a bunion or bum knee passed down the petriline. Still, from one of his spare apartments some or all of these took place:

Fireworks. Stoppedatgunpoint explorations of Oxley Road. Property churn. Torrential gains. Waking up from a dream to watch a witch wail at the window to wake up from a dream. Walkman still serving *Where The Streets Have No Name* from the tarmac following a brief carinduced flight, distressing no machine parts, no reprimand. Templemob bottlenecks on holydays. AAMembersonly arcadeban exceptionalism ('1943', 'Contra', 'Galaga '88', 'Street Fighter') after saving up enough coinage, because nochange says the stern guard, eyeout for videogameabetted gangsterism as reported in the papers. A-Levels. Swimmarches to Yong An Park along the discontinguous pavement. Wheelchair parade on verandahs and lobbies, eyes daubed by war blankstaring Beemers and swimmingpooled lofts as at Andromeda.

Narratives congeal. Not nostalgia in the sense of wantingback, but how things turn thankfully strange if taken far enough. The old man's rosewood chairs—vintage, uncushioned, beyond price—all we had to sit on.

1.415016,103.836672 (1991–1996)

Khatib calling. Take on faith that things look up, *hinterland* means *north*, that there be new stations soon. And here it is. Far from grace but near to the old action. Sembawangsoclose means cheap CDs, the last hotspring but have to show IC to the armyguard to soak, seafood. Also affordable golf for the masses. These days (circa 2017) 'home to cat abuse, murder, car chases, brothel raids, civilians trying to attack policemen with stun guns, loan sharks, falling concrete slabs, sinkholes, feuding taxi drivers, shopping mall stabbings and more', but also wanttokeepdontwanttospendtime sheltie being walked around the manmade slope. Catchnothing weekends at the fishing pier, one eye out for stray longrange bulletspeed tees, because whattodo share airspace lah, richpooroknotbad clustering for economic warmth, spillover security. Until comehome find Sister prepared to go to war rather than co-locate. Realty shows. Seventhmonth songrallies. Eighthmonth mooncake bingefairs. Year end/start red canreuse streamers for Christmas/NewYear/Valentine's declare the pasarmalam season open. *What's the point of Northpoint?* It sparked the whole suburban mall thing, it happened here, originstory of the hollowing out of Orchard Road. Might still occur, that onsen, just please not *Syonan Spa*. Had Seletaris caught on as tonic, not condo. Imagine keeping Nee Soon later, not rendered mandarin, cheerful. The baffled wellness tourists amid the builtup ashrams. The sofabed upon which much recreation and unhearddoorbell lasttime tasted, soon seniorscorner common wealth. Whole lives sprung now never having seen rubber trees, from soil once thick with nothingbut, dense with dark, riflecrack seedbursts, somesay tigers (unlikely), torchglow the only ward against fearbark, tripfallbreakleg, feedfamily biopiracy, loss. The one that refused to be cut down, even for George IV, the keramat tree, the last post, the kampung mosque, the country club community centre, the tropicana sports bar, the family steakhouse, the fishball noodles, the zhichar low, the carpark with too many mynahs, the drive to Bedok and to Gombak, the shortcut avenues, the sidetracks and bytheways branching off from the main trunks, better watch them. How long more before memoirie approaches fiction. Before words dry of sap.

1.311153,103.794883 (1998-2015)

Even built a windmill, even though then known not to be netherlandic but named after 'an architect and an amateur actor' (firstname: hugh). But with firstthought gummier than factis, who heeds dry whatwas? Whose holland then? Whose veridical? The market. The mandarin. The moment's manifold. Loudmusic next to lebanese. Chic cambodian incense atomised through airvents to burke bavarian brauhaus bouquet. The owner of original sin saying, en passant, *I charge $18 for a salad. How much more do you think I can raise prices* just so the landlord can collect kpis. Thambi peddling streetcorner newsoftheworld, any tastescriptlayoutlanguage setting *for as long as I can remember.* This atmos. This brume. This 人气. This angin, without anger mostly, more freneticalm, a kind of determination to seenotsee, to stride past the faketouts and flagsellers en route to a facial. The justheretohaveagoodtimewhycannot tilt of the chin. A goto, not a from. A place pronow.

1.310721,103.79796 (2003-2015)

What of the world's place in us? No language without air or friction. No here to be was the I. How the koel woke us calling for its mate. Or a mate. Love being what outthere we make interior. You were not and then you were and then you will be not, but not in this draw breath be told all how of it, what what made you of this. Something of these sundry streets, then, that we walked down, you colicky, to calm you, me singing. The lined lamps, the darkened windows, the cars, the cracks, the favourite corner to turn back, the fallen mangoes pecked by bats, the rotting moment sweet in their small mouths. As mightaswell as any speck of us. What is is for, you reckon. We happened to each other. Here. I'll stop herenow.

MUMBAI

before 14th April, 2014 6:42:17 pm

POOJA NANSI

UTC+5:30 • 18°57'N / 72°50'E

Songs of exile

These are the songs of parting. The songs of exile. Self imposed, or otherwise. The sound of a pen scratching as my father signs a document which says 'Renunciation of Indian nationality is irrevocable and due care must be exercised in making an application for this purpose. A declaration must be made that the renunciation is voluntary and that the applicant understands its consequences.' These are the songs of parting. A line that says 'After renunciation, you will be given a letter stating that your Indian passport has been cancelled and that you are no longer an Indian citizen.' These are the songs of exile. Self imposed or otherwise. This is how you are expected to dust the earth off you, stop looking back and make yourself (some say) a better home on foreign soil. This is how you grow up singing the songs of one land and are then supposed to forget the notes. These are the soft songs of parting, the winds different, the smells different, but the never ebbing longing always a constant flow. This is when you are always home. This is when you are never home. This is how borders of love and loyalty are expected to shift, as though your heart understands this redrawn cartography, as though country is merely movements of tectonic plates. As though country is a thing, not a feeling. As though my country can never be two places, six people, seven things. But these are the rules they say, these are the rules of exile, the songs of parting that haunt and some things we cannot translate.

Tell me the story

There's so many Bombays I do not know will not know would die to know but could never know even if I time travelled, whiskey marvelled, mused unsettled, left untitled, even if I puzzled over, battled with every punctuation pause in every family story and said no no wait no hold on what happened before that and then where did they walk to how fast did they walk and what year was this how high in the sky was the sun beating down or did monsoon soak their conversation and who heard them and how did you find out are there any photos any telegrams and could we call Raman Masi and find out if she remembers her name alright fine what colour was her dress and what did she have for breakfast and I know they fell in love that day but was it on a stomach filled with toast and eggs and no I do not know the Cathedral of the Holy Name oh was it the church we passed in Colaba but did it look the same when they stood in front of it in what year did you say it was in that record store in Kala Ghoda where we went childhoods ago to buy cassette tapes playing those Mohd Rafi songs those sad longing songs so much sad longing I thought it would flood the streets that you walked when you were eighteen and you are now sixty three and the record store is closed but we can still go to the Cathedral of the Holy Name I don't know the bends on the streets and where is this Bombay of my father's young man dreams how many right turns before I get there, no no wait no hold on what happened next?

Silverscreen

There's the Bombay of my grandparent's youth. The city I dream of time traveling to, of the silver screen and short sari pallus, of the beehives and the beaded purses, of black rimmed glasses and three piece suits. Of love stories full of absolutes and innocence—when movies were a kind of deliverance.

 I glimpse it when my grandmother sings to an old song on the radio, the gravel and warble in her vocal chords hidden by her paper thin skin give way to a young girl's glint in her eyes. Suddenly there is revelation: time is not something held in clocks. Suddenly there is burst of poetry, and the excavation of raw, chafed longing. A panoramic swish of exotic locations like Darjeeling and Kathmandu. This was before New Zealand, before the Swiss Alps before the woman in silver shimmying in Xanadu. This is tender *desh ki dharti* glamour turned into cinematic novella, my grandmother is humming to the song picturised on Manoj Kumar and Mala Sinha. I want her to never stop singing, even when she cannot hit the notes. I want to tell her, amidst the jewels and stars on the TV screen, her voice is the only thing that glows.

Amitabh Bachan

I want to marry him I whisper into the TV as a three-year-old because who else can open a car door handle like this tall swaggalicious man who else chews on a toothpick like a hot first kiss and it's hard to find words to articulate the whirlpool in my belly, his eyes that mourn but turn mourning into something sexy. Whose voice is chocolate bubbling baritone, he strolls slow while other men are falling in the middle of curry western movie fight scenes and oh my god is he puffing at that cigarette or trying to create an orgasm this man this six foot two pillar of desire ...

And the bad guy says:
'Now you're in trouble, you rogue, we've been looking for you.'
But he? He tilts his head back, exhales smoke and says:
'You've been looking all over, while I was right here waiting.'
And when *he* goes looking for the bad guy he stands like a rock in the middle of a hurricane and spits
Agar apni maa ka doodh piya hai to saamne aa.
Dammmmn son ...
you're going to make a girl unable to walk straight your smirk hits hard like a double vodka and gin cocktail. You so beautiful on a motorcycle, hard and lean on a horse. You dancing but only moving one muscle. You drenched to curve of chest in rainfall, you gun cocked with half smile. You full of anger and tenderness and sex, you aviator sunglasses, wide collared, bell bottomed styled.

God help brown girls like me everywhere growing up watching you on screens.

God help my brown girl's hunger and my brown girl's sweltering dreams.

Kum Kum Terrace revisited

Since you were a little girl you imagined bringing the man you married here. It is on this building's front steps that you invented games of secret places, passwords, patterns. Somewhere on its pillars if you scrape away yearly layers of paint are markings of your height from no movie ticket required to very small even for a six year old. This is the banister you slid down after ringing doorbells and running away. This is the railing on which you rested your head and cried because some childhood demand had not been met. This plaster and concrete two story map of your heart. And yet, here you are walking up the same stairs with his hand in yours understanding there are some parts of you, so quiet, so secret, so deep, there are no passwords for another to learn.

Mami

Mami died two days ago. She was close to ninety. One of the last living links to Kum Kum Terrace's glory days, when this two story building was bustling with the smells of everyone's cooking. When lunch was a communal affair. Chappatis from apartment 3, raita from 5 upstairs, bhindi from number 4 and my grandmother's daal made in her pocket sized kitchen in number 2. The doors always open, their borderless thresholds. As children, we would nap in anyone's house, everyone had the keys to the neighbours, some of your pots were inevitably on the shelves next door and would never come back to you empty.

But vessels rust, shelves sag, children grow up, move away, old friends and neighbours age and disappear. An old woman is left behind performing the same routine of incense sticks, medicated soaps, cumin seeds, flower garlands, deep heat. The paint on her walls crumbling, the pipes corroding, the linen yellowed. She smiles when you knock on her door 20 years older, looks at your husband and tells him, 'we knew her when she was this small'. Her shriveled hands held apart, the small length of a still ticking watch.

Bharti

Bharti steals from the pantry my aunt hisses at me when the cook is out of reach. *The other time there was only enough flour left for three rotis ... I do not know where the potatoes are disappearing.* Bharti smiles a decayed toothless grin but she has fed generations on convalescent food, festive meals, baby mush. Bharti folds samosas like her hands are in rush hour traffic. She slips in and out of houses *what is for dinner what is for lunch how much daal should be soaked how much vegetable should be cooked how much do we portion out without spice how much curd should be mixed with the rice.* Bharti measures and weighs her life in pinched fingers of atta and oil and onions and ghee, she measures time in pressure cooker whistles and the serving of tea. The pallu of Bharti's saris are tucked into her waist and sometimes when nobody is looking she takes a little flour, a little meat, a little cumin, a little fish. These are the only manifestations of desire, the only dreams that still exist. She listens in the sizzle of a frying pan for some lost prophecy.

In Bharti's own peeling kitchen there are empty vessels where the answers should be.

Geeta Cinema

Ten steps away from Kum Kum Terrace is the Geeta Cinema, where you can watch B grade movie reruns and buy tickets in black from the men outside chanting inflated prices under their breath. I write letters to my grandfather and label the envelope *2 Kum Kum Terrace, Geeta Cinema Compound*. A midnight movie adventure is only five minutes away. Where you can sit on the wooden slatted seat, eat channa, drink Limca and lose yourself in somebody else's dream. Where grandmothers live forever and never lose their memory; where the bad guys find their comeuppance and the tall dark hero emerges victorious; where you are the heroine, her spangled dupatta reflecting off her long dark hair; where a song seals a romance and your long lost father is a benevolent billionaire. Where rain drenches you but your make up never runs; where alcohol is a river that never gets you drunk. Where everyone always wants to dance and always knows the steps where nobody has heard of a smartphone or e-books or a multiplex.

What I didn't say when I told Shane about buying a plane ticket to watch Bryan Adams live in Mumbai, February 12th, 2011.

What could I tell him about the nights I have spent with you? That Indian summer night I decided to sleep naked and discovered a place inside me to the sound of your voice. The times the girls at school made fun of me for hairy legs, thick eyebrows, how I came home broken inside and there you were on MTV—playing your guitar and I wondered if I would ever be pretty enough for anyone to hold me like that, play me like that. And how you tilted your head to the chords, smiled a half smile like there was a secret between us, and how the next day, I would float, float, float out of my grief and run to you in a dream, how I would walk lost in the memory of your lips, your voice like silk wrapped gravel, hard and gentle the way years later, I would learn to love to be touched.

You sing, you sing you sing you sing you sing you sing you sing to my loneliness and you say it's ok hush darling, it's ok, hush, it will be alright. You sing and I am like a cracking egg, all liquid inside. You sing, you wring the heart of me, you fix everything, you are what spring does to the cherry trees, you unhinge me, you sing and I am drowning, I am vulnerable and uncoiling. Now you are crooning husky, now you are serenading, you are laughing, now you are guitar lovemaking.

What can I tell him about your voice and my yearning how do I make a poem from feelings I don't know the names of, where do I find words for the moments more important than desire? How do I tell him with you I will always be twelve, insecure and inhibited, that there is no aging, you are not a person, you are boat in wide ocean, you are safe passage.

What could I tell him about how I first learnt to love myself by loving you?

Flight SQ 422 Singapore to Mumbai, listening to Nusrat Fateh Ali Khan upon landing

Yours is the music of quiet four a.m., of solitary afternoons, the music of desire, the exhale of the Urdu word for 'need', like the sound of a lung first learning breath, or the shape of my father's mouth turning into song. Yours the voice of sandpaper and husk, like the call for God coming from a garbage truck throat, the voice of surrender, surrender to the longing of living, to all bottomless need to be filled, to find another, to be whole. Yours the poet's knowledge of how to moan a word, the low humming of all the world's restless stirring, the yearning, the always and forever yearning, the trembling lips of a muted string waiting to burst. Yours the hunger of a fakir who has forsaken begging to shout from the rooftops. Yours the sweet wine of grief, the unbridled intoxication which you deliver like a lover's return, the notes that land like a hand tapping on the tight drumskin of my heart, then the strum of the harmonica which struggles to keep up with your voice. Yours the utterance of devotion, the prophet's chant, the treacherous winding road harmony, the fevered ecstasy. Yours a wild animal wail from before words, the sound of the soul freed of the ribcage, from some ancient deep forgotten history, every exuberant end, every troubled beginning.

MOSCOW

1974

SUBHASH JAIRETH

UTC+3 • 55°45'N / 37°37'E

The climb to the top of the trampoline tower is hard. I lead and you follow which is new for both of us. Soon the sun will rise, you mumble. The platform shudders. We look and see the blue coaches of the metro rush through the station on the bridge across the river. Soon the sun will rise, you murmur again, standing on the platform. We wait for the sun to come out from behind the early morning clouds. It doesn't; its emergence usurped by drizzle that soon turns into rain. It falls into the water in the river, gently at first and then in big splashes. The water in the river begins to shake as if someone has put the water in a jar and given it a mighty stir. A ferry appears blowing its horn and emitting clouds of stinking smoke. We hear the engine's heavy chug chug chug bounce off the hill and echo back. But before it fades, the rough crowing of ravens shatters the beat. The birds circle the platform a few times and disappear. The rain stops. In the dim wet light of the sun the city begins to reveal itself.

It's quite late at night and the night is bright like a summer day; and summer it is, the summer of 1974. The tram moves slowly, tired, half asleep. You open the case, take out your violin and stand near the driver's cabin. In the tram there is just one more passenger: an old woman with a red scarf. You start playing: a polonaise of Schubert. The tram stops and I see the driver come out of the cabin. She is a young woman, heavily pregnant. She stands leaning against the railing. You finish the polonaise and we applaud; bravo, the old woman says; the driver picks up a carnation lying on the dashboard and gives it you. You accept the flower, bow, and ask her if you can touch her belly. The driver agrees. You touch, smile and whisper words I can't hear.

...

In the market you stop at a stall and start talking to an old woman selling mandarins from Morocco. You talk to her as if you had known each other for years. I watch transfixed by the earring dangling from your left ear urging my hand not to move to touch. He loves you, I hear the old woman tell you. I know, you say. He is stupid. No, he isn't, she says, and hands you a little bag of mandarins. She asks you your name. Tamrico from Tbilisi, you reply. *Tsarmatebebi* (good luck), she says offering you a bunch of irises from the table of her neighbour. *Gmadlobt'* (thank you), you reply. Let's go, you say and we rush outside. At the station you drop the irises in the bin, look straight at me and pronounce: they were for the daughter we would never have.

...

The boy is only four or perhaps a little older. He stands with his mother looking at the painting. There isn't any one around in the hall. The figure in the painting holds a bright sun-like ball in her hands. Her eyes are shut but her face glows in the light. *The Gift of Friendship* it is called. I watch and listen. The boy hesitates. His mother prompts. I can't hear the words but their whispers waft in the air. They look at each other and smile. I leave the gallery without looking at other paintings. Outside the gallery I see you sitting on the steps. As I take my place next to you, I notice a picture postcard in your hand. The card has the same painting on it. We look and only then a thought flashes in my mind. The young woman I saw was perhaps you and I was the four-year-old boy looking at the sun-like ball ready to accept the luminous gift. But who was the woman holding the ball in the painting? Ask Ciurlionis, you say, he painted her.

...

Can I take your photo? You ask the nurse. Of course, she replies. She asks me to join her seated on the bench with her friends. The woman is a retired army nurse. The friend to her right was a pilot and the other man with dark hair and twinkle in his eyes is an Armenian who had driven his tank all the way to Berlin. Before shaking hands the tank-driver pulls out a photo from his pocket. Berlin, he says, and the three scribble their names on the back of the photo. We look and want to ask about the young man who was with them in Berlin when the photo was shot. Vovka, Vera the nurse speaks. He was nineteen and died two days after the photo was taken; killed by a roadside mine. As she gives me the photo she touches the face of Vovka with her hand. And then from nowhere a young man with a *garmoshka* appears. He plays and the three break into a dance. That's when I see you nod and we slowly walk away from the fountain outside the Bolshoi Theatre.

...

There are five eggs in the basket. All painted hematite red. The nun wants me to take one. I can't decide. They look perfect where they are. If I pick one the four remaining would appear odd. I wait for you to make the first move but you don't. The nun stands still. Silent. Forbearing. A smile unfolds the wrinkles of her face. It ripples and I hear it roll like water on the white beech sand. The nun takes an egg and drops in your hand. It has a white birch leaf painted on it. Now I do have to pick one before the Nun chooses one for me. But you beat her to it. This is for you, you say. The yellow oak leaf painted on it glimmers for a moment. The nun hurriedly marks a sign of the cross in the air, looks around to check if we are being watched, and shuffles away. The bells in the church tower remain silent. A jogger runs past followed by two cyclists. We stop to give way to a duck heading for the pond followed by five of her brood. I put my hand inside the pocket of your parka. The egg feels warm. Your hand cold. It's going to rain you say although there isn't a speck of cloud in the bluest of blue skies. Yes, it will, I reply and the game we play with each other drags on.

...

I love the blue onion-shaped dome I want to say. You don't, you can't, I hear as if you had caught the sound of thought before it had left my mind. And so we stand not far from the entrance to the New Donskoi Cemetery. *Blokhin, Vasili Mikhailovich* I read the name on the gravestone. Read again, you ask. I comply. He killed my grandfather, you say. Misho Alavidze, my mother's father. That night in July 1940 one hundred and twenty eight were shot; each with a bullet from a German Walther. He liked the low calibre weapon. It made no or little mess to clean. To wash the powder he had alcohol and vodka he couldn't live without. For blood he had just water he didn't like the touch of. He was a proud *Chekist*, honoured for his service and silence. Silence reigned in the house as well where he returned each morning to say *Dobroe Utro* to his wife; to kiss her and be kissed. Tell me about Misho, I ask. Not here, not now, you say and we walk out of the cemetery watched by a pair of blackbirds perched on the gravestone.

...

Kuznetskii Most, the street where Mayakovskii begged the fallen horse to get on its feet, is a bridge, you say. Over here, near the lamp post, a young woman standing next to us, points the spot. Like this, she slumps on the wet from the snow cobble stones. Please don't, I want to say but she is keen to enact the scene. An old man, his face painted white, kneels down beside the sprawled figure of the woman. The man begins to speak; his falsetto voice slashes the stiffened air: *listen to me dear horse. Don't do this to us. Don't you think my little one that there is a bit of horse in all of us; that we are in our own way nothing but horses? Have mercy on us my dear. Forgive us if you can.* He raises his arms. His head slumps as if broken at the neck. The crowd sighs. But then the woman rouses herself; mounts on the back of her companion and the two leave clomping on the cold stones. I wait hoping for her to turn and look back. We have to go, you mumble. But just before we step away glass beads from someone's necklace fall on the stones and roll like marbles.

I just need a prompt, he says, and the mind projects a map I need to trace my walk in the city. Venice, I ask him, and he draws a picture of two hands clasped together. Leningrad, I challenge, and it reappears like a triple-head python. Alexandria has the shape of an ibis lying on brown sand washed by the turquoise waters of a warm sea. Brasilia reminds him of an eagle flying down from a hill ready to land in the lake to take a dip. And what about Moscow? I ask. It's like you, he says, and draws the map on my body; his fingers tracing seven mounds and hills cut through by rivers and streams.

I ask him about the swallows I see drawn on the sketches of buildings he shows me. To add colour, he says. That he is lying is clear to me as well as to him; the lie confirms the truth I already know. There are two swallows on the roofs of Melnikov's Cylinder; three on the Planetarium and five above the dome of the Pioneer Palace; but there is none on the Lenin Mausoleum. The one on the arch of the metro station is blue-green. This is you, he confesses at last. I know, I say. They all are you; without you nothing is complete. *Chepukha* (what nonsense!), I wince. Like Calvino's Marco Polo he wants to trace the invisible parabolas the swallows cut in the air. Without them the skies are hollow, he says, and cities unhomely.

...

He is surprised by the map I have found for him. He wants to know if I am a mind reader. No, I say but like the swallow in your drawing of the metro station I know how to hop inside your mind and fly parabolas in the dreamscape it conjures. And play violin? He asks. Perhaps, I reply. A swallow with a violin: the image makes us smile. We know that we are afflicted by the same sickness the name of which is Chagall. Only he can make the cows fly, the goats sing; and the red apple kiss your lips, he adds.

...

The map I gave him has entered a scrapbook he calls the *Book of Forgetting and Remembering*. To forget being with you isn't hard, he says, but the remembrance of being without you hurts. He has cut the map into pieces and pasted them on separate pages. Each piece floats in the sea littered with detritus of our walks together: a silver button from a blouse, a blue feather of a bird, brown seeds of an apple, a piece of string of my violin, a large photo of an earlobe with a pearly stud, a validated tram-ticket, a sharp wedge of a Japanese vase, a chip of a painted egg shell, et cetera ... et cetera ...

...

What's this? I ask pointing at the blood spot on a sharp wedge of a vase. Remains, he says, of your present I bought from *Beryozka* (the foreign currency store). He opens the backpack and spreads on the floor fragments: the round narrow neck, three pieces of a flat bottom and many more. Picks up a pen, draws the shape on a sheet and waits. Let us put it back, his eyes plead. What for? A little shrug of the shoulder, a hesitant smile followed by an inaudible moan; he knows it won't happen. There was a pigeon, he says, right above Mayakovskii's marble head. He had stopped, as he always does, in the metro station, to stand for a moment near the bust and read to the poet words of his poem about the star-lit sky. The pigeon dropped from the roof, hit his hand and the vase slipped. A young boy helped him gather the pieces. His name is Misha (I mishear Misho). He is ten and loves figure skating. And what about the pigeon? I ask. Misha took it home to his mother, he says. Tamara (I mishear Tamrico) is a nurse. His voice quivers and that's when I notice two strips of band-aid on his left hand. The blood on the wedge could be his or of the pigeon. I don't ask and he doesn't proffer an answer.

...

The *Tsar-Kolokol* (Tsar-Bell) is silent; has always been and will remain so. Inside the bell lies the severed *Yzyk* (tongue), its clapper. Settled on the sandstone pedestal the bell mocks its bell-ness ringing aloud the silence we too have imposed on ourselves. We are damaged like the bell, you say, and point the large bronzy wound gaping at us without mercy or remorse. The broken slab stands nearby unwilling to cover the darkness inside the cavernous hole. The bell was too heavy to be raised. To drag it out of the clay pit was impossible. The experiment failed then and it will fail again. We know it will because we live a failed dream; a nightmare for dreamers like Misho, my silly old *Babua* (grandfather). I hear you lament and for a moment wish a white dove to appear from inside the dark belly of the bell and land on your shoulder. It will brush your neck with its wings, coo and crackle, and then fly off, leaving us marooned but happy.

...

Here is my Babua Misho, you say handing me a photo. A young man in the Red Army uniform stands in the shadow of a crumbling bell tower. His foot next to the shattered head of a marble statue holding in his arms an icon. He was twenty-nine then, a faithful foot soldier of *Tovarish* (Comrade) Stalin. It took weeks to bring down the *Khram* (Cathedral) but more than a year to remove the debris. Christ the Saviour, for whom the *Khram* was built, couldn't save His own temple. The marble Mayakovskii you like so much was carved probably from the rock retrieved from the rubble. The same rubble was raided for stones to reinforce the walls of Donskoi Cemetery where lie the ashes of Misho interned in a mass grave, unnamed, unmarked. Each time the name Misho is pronounced your face turns ashen white; the voice flattens and your eyes want to look away. A Palace of the Soviets was supposed to replace the *Khram* but it was too heavy for the clayey base near the river to stand on. So the hole was filled for us to swim and forget the ugly tale. Now you know why you seem to hear the church bells ringing when you float on your back in the warm waters of the pool.

...

He has found the exact place where Doctor Zhivago died. Is this really important? I ask. Not really, he replies but the disappointment in his voice is hard to ignore. He died in the book I could have said to tease him even more. I also know the tram routes A and B which Mandelshtam wrote into his poem, he says. And to convince me he pulls out an old 1931 route map of Moscow trams. He has a friend he says, an architect like him, who has connections. He calls the man Igor, the octopus, with tentacles able to unlock secret vaults. To cheer him up I agree to walk with him to the spot near the Moscow Zoo. But the walk doesn't happen. I am called by my dear aunt in Tbilisi to help her care for her husband suffering from dementia. I'll come back, I tell him but he doesn't believe. Each time we part, he says, we part forever; something of us never returns or whatever returns appears estranged.

The autumn this year is glorious. If this is to compensate for your absence I want it to return to the restrained beauty of yesteryears. Each day I take the metro to Kolominkskoe to sketch churches and izbas (cottages); the same places I had sketched a year earlier when you were with me. I have now finished three pairs of 'with-you' and 'without-you' landscapes. I look at them and can't decide which of the two appeases me more. In a recent dream I saw you walk in and out of the sketched landscapes with such ease that it felt as if in my dream they were not drawings but real natural landscapes. And I heard your violin. Not Schubert but Bach. The same chaconne you played once in the shadow of Pushkin one late very late night. Just a coincidence you would have said. Yes, a coincidence it was. No more words I warn myself. No compulsion to remember or forget. Let the unsaid remain unasked, untranslated, untouched.

HAIFA

171-173 B.E.

NILOOFAR FANAIYAN

UTC+2 • 32°49'N / 35°00'E

Arriving

She's on the night train again—luggage stored between seats and in the aisles—she loses track of the stops, where passengers board and disembark, and in between a soldier naps cradling her assault rifle, a couple of students sketch in their art books while charging their mobile phones, and restless youths traipse up and down looking for optimum seating. The first change she notices is the feeling of approach, the heightened sense, the surface numbing around the temples that marks the traversing of ley lines, the drawing nigh to a place of pilgrimage—soon, as she peers through the windows on the left, she can see a shoreline and a tumult of waves, and as she takes a deep breath and looks through the windows on the right, she sees the lights of suburbia, the lights of industry, the lights of a city, and the lights of the mountain, a golden dome in the middle of the northern slope.

December

Fairy-lights on Ben Gurion get confused with fireworks on Abbas and the parties on both streets are going on long past midnight. Earlier in the evening the ethereal sound of nuns singing in Arabic mingles with the call to prayer—the two rabbis perched in front of Netzach Israel Synagogue are having some sort of theological debate with a determined pair of youngsters —a few days later and it's the same pair of youngsters wearing new sets of clothing. The Muslim restaurateur on Allenby is busy serving his Christian and Jewish neighbours on holiday, calling them all by name—on Friday he goes out to eat at a place owned by one of those same neighbours. Guards and volunteers chat to visitors as they enter the Bahá'í gardens, and tourists take selfies with the terraces behind them. The sweet smell of hot sufganiyot being pulled from bakery ovens makes the children frantic, and the rich fragrance of cardamom and coffee wafts through the alleys—the rain (much needed and prayed for) pauses for a few days, the sky clears and the air bites, and in the distance sits Mount Hermon dressed in jagged snow.

Bus stop on Hatzionut

There's a bus stop on Hatzionut, by a wall of stone bricks, where street lights glow a soft golden and the whooshing of passing traffic mingles with the whisper of souls. They pass through the gaps in the bushes that sit atop the stone, a second softer wall that holds the garden in its embrace. Two young girls, chatting and laughing, at the end of a long day, skip past a car parked over the kerb on the corner of Shifra, one of them has a pink hibiscus tucked behind her ear—hibiscus dangle through and over the fence on the other side, almost red in the lamplight, nodding at the whispering souls. The girls pause, quietly looking over the wall over their shoulders, then continue their trek up the mountain. Behind them a bus stops on Hatzionut.

Soundscape

the sound of horns being blown as another ship leaves the harbour, as cars converge in less-time traffic, and the clanging of bottles and bits of metal as cats rush through alleyways to avoid the children out from school, and the rustling of palm leaves as an afternoon wind pushes clouds over the Mediterranean, and the clicking of cypress needles as the same wind gets tangled in the gardens, and the ringing of church bells muffled by a flock of hooded crows flying in formation, and the undulating melody of the adhan coasting with the eagles coasting overhead and calling to each other, and the chatter of shop owners and neighbours and passers-by that pauses only with the breaking of the sound barrier, and the rhythmic music that lifts-off with sunset and is occasionally drowned by fireworks, farewells and arrivals, and the whoosh of trains pulling in and out of Merkaz HaShmona, and the sound of horns being blown as another ship leaves the harbour.

Der Herr ist Nähe 1

Someone engraved it into stone over a hundred years ago—the stone is now grey and the window shutters are an old teal, and no-one remains who might have seen the house built or the stone engraved. On the other side of the mountain worshippers tread the floor of a cave inside a chapel inside Stella Maris monastery—the cave walls are glossy as though the oils of many fingers and palms have been rubbed across the rocky interior —someone lights a candle at the simple altar, next to a stack of papers and pencils. They take a paper and pencil and write a prayer, scrunch up the prayer, find a crack or crevice in the wall, feed the tiny ball of paper to the belly of the cave, back out of the alcove, ducking their head with an additional prayer to the Prophet Elijah, and re-enter the gold and mural-covered room of the church—on the other side of the mountain, within a circle of cypress, a young man lifts up his head and sees fire in the sky.

Der Herr ist Nähe 2

The cobblestones on Ha-Parsim dance with flickering memories, with the heavy tread of tortured feet, with the light frolic of well-loved youth, the careful footfall of age, the quick stride of a new world, the reverent steps of travel-weary suppliants, filled with longing and consumed by separation. The plodding of donkeys echoes in the gutters and close behind follows the cart carrying grains and rice, carrying visitors from the port, bulletins, notes, and letters carrying the fragrance of love and assistance from friends from far away. The cobblestones dance to a music from within the walls, a music of all-time and no-time, a music that is prayer in its intonation in its incantation in its seeming silence—and near the intersection is a house of old stone with an engraving over old teal shutters, 'Der Herr ist Nähe'.

Moon over Haifa Bay

She hovered by the circle of cypress trees standing tall and still in the calm—a yellow moon rose over the bay and drowned the mountain, the sea seemingly rose lifting the ships at rest into a softly tilting lullaby. As the second verse started the trees began to murmur sage-wood scented harmonies that wafted through the windows on HaGefen and meandered along the foot of Carmel, and at 3 a.m. a breeze from beyond the bay joined the chorus. Layers of voices lifted into a crescendo from across time —the voice of Elisha Roman conquerors Greek fisherman Arab traders Christian crusaders Ottoman rulers German Templers Jewish settlers British soldiers—and then the pilgrims stepped to the fore, as she lifted the baton and brought in the sunrise.

The beach

There's a stretch of yellow sand along the coast of Haifa, between the train tracks and the sea. A giant billboard of a camel marks the carpark's entrance—I could feel my shoulders burning slowly as I walked in the summer sun, the air murky with humidity, the sea foam hovering, then evaporating. You can see cargo ships and cruise ships move in and out of the bay, the traffic typically busy at the edge of the Mediterranean—the waves typically busy for the edge of the season—I sat in the shade and sipped a limunana, the tang of lemon cutting into my tongue. Boats that couldn't make it to the port once landed on the beach, travellers resting under the palm trees, the mountain a not-too-distant beacon. I was waiting for the right moment, the instant when the sun hits the water just so, when the waves roll back into a choppy Mediterranean blue—has the sea always been this crowded, this used? A camera leapt into my fingers and the wind picked up speed.

Across the bay

A circling coastline captures the tumultuous deep, swells of seawater break against anchored ships, break on the pillars of the port, break on the rocks of the northern shore, fall on southern sands and crash against sea walls—two hundred and fifty years later the seawater worries that wall—a back and forth movement, like the people in cars and sheruts on the highway between Haifa and Akka, as though they are one city not two, as though each is a lodestone—the people are drops of liquid mercury hovering between. Some have forgotten what the walls to the north once contained, some have forgotten that the mountain to the south was arid for the longest time, but the sea keeps digging away—and as a circling coastline captures and holds the deep, the mountain gazes north across the bay at the prison by the sea.

And then it rains

The gnarled branches, extending from a great twisting body, reach out to the world in all directions, with glossy sage-like leaves—she stretches deep into the mountain and no-one knows how long she has lain there. A black-and-white mottled cat lies in her shadow, staying out of the sun and away from other cats—a gardener checks the branches for any fruit and moves on. The haze is shifting on the horizon, the desert dust almost tangible in the air—the birds overhead break formation and the cat runs for greater shelter. Someone crushes her fallen leaves underfoot in the rush for cover—the smell of olive oil is lifted by the dusty wind, and then it rains.

CAPE TOWN

1962 to 2002

JEN WEBB

UTC+2 • 33°55'S / 18°25'E

The mother city

You had forgotten everything. The tree-lined streets with tree names: Protea Road, Woodlands Road, Silvertree Lane. Tourists snapping pictures of heritage homes, of bronze lions on permanent watch halfway up Devil's Peak. Going home: this is where you began, born into harsh history. The brightly painted slave quarters at Bo-Kaap. How the children fled giggling from the ragged men. The night the soldiers came.

Muizenberg Beach

White sharks surfing beyond their steel-net walls. Candy-cane changing sheds where the walls are clammy and the floors are clammy and the smell is of genteel decay. They are not hers, but she owns everything between them and the sea: gold sand that burns beneath her feet; green water that in daylight breaks into lace and at night phosphoresces into Catherine wheels, turning her skin to light. That is hers, and the beach umbrellas canted at the right angle: they are hers too. And the ice cream men ringing their bells, and the children asking for coins. When she stands on the edge of the beach, and roars, even the sea loses its nerve.

Fishing

He ate snoek for dinner, caught fresh that morning off Kalk Bay and bought from a boy who leaned toward him across the fishing boat, holding up fingers to say how much. The snoek, shining, the colour of steel. The boat too was shining steel, half pulled up on sand where each new breath and sigh of the sea rocked it back on its heels. Further out, boys on boards were weaving patterns between the waves. Further still, container ships moved across a mirror and then dropped, one by one, off the edge of the world. He skinned the snoek and grilled it, and ate it with sweet potatoes and onions, and a good red he had set to breathe earlier that day. She has gone, has taken her golden limbs and her breathless passion and the way she wept, inconsolable, her back turned to him, and for all he knows she has dropped off the edge of the world.

Near False Bay

Everything is moving. On the drive-in screen a girl whirls, en pointe, a scattered light. The hill beyond careers to the shore and plunges into water, aiming at a ragged line where the Indian Ocean, whip-stitched to the Atlantic, tugs at the seam. You raise your hand and lay a finger along your third eye. I can no longer reach you. On the screen, the story shifts: you stand, and light is thrown across you: a horse gallops between your shoulder blades; its rider lifts a sword, and I feel the knife in my own back. The wind whips in from the beach with the scent of dead fish and the muted roar of mismatched oceans, as close as memory.

Robbeneiland

We took the ferry from the harbour, out beyond where seals colonise the bay. The water was dark and busy, rips wrestling the swell. There is a line in the sea there, where oceans meet. Rocks mark the spot. Other children turned green and leaned across the rails, ribboning vomit into the sea. The crew washed the deck with seawater, drenching our shoes. I shook water from my feet and picked up my box brownie. The rock ahead of us; its prison walls, the sea birds calling into the gale. The camera shook. The photos failed.

Robben Island

We took the ferry, out beyond the breakers. Green water arched its back, the boat bellyflopping from swell to swell, and seabirds guided us in through the rocks. You climbed the breakwater, measuring against the sea our public shame. The guns are gone, and the guards. No birds remember that old rough game, and if the stones know, or the sea, they have no tongues to talk. History bites back, all the same. We stood apart, strangers, in the punishment yards. Later I reached for you, your skin on mine, your living breath.

Bergvliet

In tadpole season we bunked off school, heading for the slow stream at the edge of the lawn. The gardener pointed us toward our prey in the shallows: shining commas, dark questions, ellipses smudged against stones. We scooped them into jars full of still water and hard light, shards of rock and scraps of weed. The tadpoles butted against the glass, and some died, and some changed, and when new frogs escaped the jars, the servants caught them and took them back to the stream. That year the nights were full of song.

Just like memory: fragments

Between Hout Bay and Clifton the plane starts a crazy dance, and then it's the smell of heat, and then it's smoke curling between our feet. The captain soothes while the cabin crew lock us down and shout safety. You reach for the stranger beside you, and refuse to consider the past. Through the porthole you spy the Apostles dressed in their cloth of cloud. Don't think aeroplanes and mountains, don't entertain worst thoughts. Remember swimming off Bloubergstrand last month, sandboarding at Mossel Bay. Taste that cigarillo you smoked last week in Moçambique, its banana-leaf skin, its gift of something wild. The aeroplane bucks and jives, the smoke rises, the mountain is near.

1960

The people fleeing the scene. A boy who carries his sister, their mouths and eyes aghast. A man weeping, a child held against his chest. The woman in her good skirt and coat. She holds a purse over her head, or she drops her purse as she runs, or she lashes out with her purse, striking the air. You saw them too, from a world away. Screens full of sorrows. Police cracking whips. The child that fell and lay still. My mother caught me up. It was not my turn that day.

1967

It was the year after the killing, it was the Six Day War, dominees threatened from their pulpits and the government cracked down. At night we locked the doors and set the wires so the windows hummed. There were storms every night, and lightning bolts lit up the alarms, as police cars wailed and the valley struggled in its chains. We stretched ourselves on courtyard benches behind the walls, watching searchlights carve the sky. We were learning the night, and learning touch. This would never be our war; we would never be the soldiers, buckling our boots, gathering our guns.

Table Mountain

The fire beating down behind you, the mountain burning, you run, a flock of panicked geese, calling out for comfort. The sky is lovely, oranges and reds, but no one stops to take pictures on a night like this. If you could pray you'd pray. You are finger puppets on someone else's hand. If you could pray, you'd imagine the great heavens opening up, wrapping you in foil. All is crackle, and pop, and cough. You pause at the foot of the mountain, at the mouth of the bay, the patient frightened geese milling around. The smell of sweat and smoke. Coughing. Bright water in sleepy waves. Seagulls yawn and stretch, the sky opens.

Rhodes Memorial

No one sleeps in the shadow of the mountain and wakes unchanged. The lions are still there, decades later, their bronze buffed by generations of kids, immune to the steep fall below and the burn of metal on skin. They gaze across the mother city, backs to the mountain, their eyes to sea where the oceans collide and boys still ride unsafe waves. She climbs her lion and straddles it, a statue on a statue. She is queen of the mountain, queen of the seas, she was born into shadow, and raised on the backs of lions. She is not afraid.

ROME

August 2015 to January 2016

PAUL HETHERINGTON

UTC+1 • 41°54'N / 12°29'E

Insomnia

1.

Rome's idling sleep is absorbed in four a.m. traffic noise; muted repetitions of music from next door; thoughts of fractious words like sleepless flies; gorgons from decades ago with mobile stone faces. Sleep's no curtain; it's a blank stare failing to close eyes; an encircling clock without hands. The waking exclamation of day will arrive and meanwhile exhaustion's imp promises its approach a hundred times. Ghosts trip on the floor, spilling entrails. I turn. The future's face is death—Goliath's head hanging from David's stretching hand. His expression invites no conversation. What have poems told me?

2.

It's a foreign city breathing closely in your ear, 'I do not care for you'. It's a different accent crawling over your beer. In daylight you liked it; now you doubt mistranslation's taste. Days have a different length; the exigencies of night won't lie straight. Your breathing sounds like alarm and there's abjection in your heart. 'Love,' you thought, but maybe you're unwell. Dis-ease accosts you as someone slams a door. The boiler hums like a perpetual motion machine—or perhaps that's the universe disaggregating light. Darkness will come like neurons winking out. If 'forever' means anything it's unwaking sleep—like espresso in a glass; like black angels painting Rome's voluminous sky.

Meeting Death

1.

This evening Death sits at the bar of *Bir and Fud* in Rome. The Belgian stout is as smooth as his conversation as he laughs about how the Roman Empire served him well. It feels like blasphemy because I'm thinking of my dear friend, but I realise this is necessary talk, where sentiment meets Death's pragmatic face. He's distracted now, talking to a young woman, and she has no idea what's coming. But neither do I—and I know who he is. He's strangely beguiling with his marvellous literary knowledge ('writers have always loved me') and his interest in historical epochs. He has an opinion about everything, which is a kind of death in itself. But I keep listening and he buys me a beer, promising it means nothing.

2.

Death leaves and the drink he promised doesn't arrive. The girl he was beguiling is eating a bowl of chips. Trastevere is still here and, so far, we've survived the night—suddenly it all feels like a minor miracle. Which, in a way, it is, and I feel my friend close, as if he's stayed to watch. It may be the blue Christmas lights strung in the street, but I think of what survives. Of my friend's final words—about love that persists. As it so often does despite every quotidian failure. Death will come back, but not yet.

A room

There's a room in which we sit. High windows, long views of a street. You hold a cold bottle and pour yellow wine. It tastes of melon and grass; it grips the tongue. 'How long?' you ask. I nod but have no answer. We'll walk outside and chase a street to a river. Green water, tumultuous cloud. Scooters that rev and subside. A gathering of stalls. You may buy underwear or a bracelet. I may try another scarf. Wind will collect our words. When we return our room will hold the day close. 'More wine?' We'll empty the bottle.

Song

The song inhabits the room like a calling back of yesterdays. Maria Callas catching sticky air, as Rome traffic seethes below. It might be the noise of love; or the sound of what was never said. It might be the other side of murmuring intimacy. We open the door to the balcony and stand among pot plants in rain. There's a crescendo of thunder; someone shouting next door. The baritone's reply rises; loss inhabits the song; a man walks out of a downstairs room and onto shining pavement. He glances left and right, a voice chasing him along a passageway.

Colours

The flea market is a longer walk than we manage and daylight's a litter of too many colours. Flusters of wind lift tarpaulins with the sound of broken applause. There are pans, sunglasses, myriad jewels—facsimiles of quality everywhere. The shells and dried starfish are stiffly real. Diaries await privacies. Etruscan artefacts are dusted with twenty-five centuries. A young woman carries a potted pomegranate and its small fruit might have been painted. A cache of strange owls peers without blinking. And, yes, we've listened to those albums. They inhabit our past like the impress of wandering hands. Who held us close on a similar carpet? Who sent us an identical lamp? We lay under its light and watched three years pass. A young couple fingers its petalled shapes as we stand in their futures.

Metronomes

When in the piazza I said to her 'stay' and she refused, a man on an awkward-looking bicycle nearly careened into us; a woman pushed past with a trolley, reaching for a glossy magazine; a boy blew soap bubbles from a plastic ring. I turned to go but she held me for a moment. Two policemen in graceful peaked hats nodded towards us. Our fingers were gentle metronomes marking time on the other's hands; her eyes were blue stones in the jewellers' window.

Misstep

This windowless room is where you might find yourself on any unexceptional day, misstepping in a palazzo's marbled corridors. Its ceiling is ornate absence; its walls are decorated with excruciated mouthings of clay, repetitious as cuneiform. Silence becomes an indecipherable shout—there's nowhere else to look, no opportunity to turn away.

Footsteps

They barely noticed their outlines in the mirror. They bought a Portuguese salad bowl and filled it with oranges. The gifts sent by a friend didn't suit the space. The apartment had a pile of CDs and the Beatles' *Love* album suited their sense of exigency. But they couldn't say what pressed them together; what climbed through their spines at night. They felt their way towards the city where an Enoteca supplied cheap tempranillo and a supermarket tray bulged with artichokes. Outside, their futures walked. At night one or other would wake, listening to the footsteps.

Accents

There was the slow turning ceiling fan that clicked at every rotation, and a box of chocolates on the scratched dark wood table. A friend's gift, and a small accompanying knife. She ran her finger on the blade, absentmindedly, and it cut her neatly in a shape like a frown. Pain tickled and sharpened. The Band-Aid barely stanched the flow. To be here in his absence was to fall into reverie; the wound reminded her of his undertakings. The view caught her, as in a glove; the friend who'd left the gift had disappointed her. And this city troubled her—as if her skin were newly vulnerable; as if her manners were suddenly gauche. In the neighbouring apartment a man fed a dog; a woman danced, a couple bickered in a rooftop garden. New accents thronged her tongue.

Saturation

In the hallway, where books were shelved according to subject, a red lamp burned. In the room itself, coffee sputtered on the stove. A woman stood like an embodiment of the uncanny, speaking strongly about ethics. Light fell from windows as if being dragged to the floor. He stood in the saturation of memory and was immobilised. He drank wine, light subsided, the city's noise dropped. The large painting on the wall lost its beauty. A spider elaborated a web and he would have disentangled it, just in that moment, when the black orb was swinging to and fro. Just then, holding himself away from knowledge, not wanting its verdict.

Hemispheres

The distances between stars are small compared to the airy hemispheres that separate us; words failing to make a bridge; daily doings unable to fortify our reduction to this dark essential. Remnant thought and feeling trundle through each week—as you did before I left Australia, shifting food about a plate, asking what noise disturbed you, bitten by pain in your legs. There's a day in November when I draft your obituary—you visit a restaurant in Rome and I can barely believe you've travelled that depth of sky. Later, looking at your final manuscripts, there's page after page missing your old inflections.

NEW ORLEANS

A Literary Tour, November 2012

CASSANDRA ATHERTON

UTC-6 • 29°57'N / 90°04'W

Kate Chopin's House, 1413 Louisiana Avenue, New Orleans, LA.

The pre-dawn hush is a votive offering as we stand looking up at the balcony's wrought iron lacework. Perhaps we don't love art or music in the same way, but we're both solitary walkers breathing in life under sleeping skies. I don't know if Degas ever met Chopin as they strolled down Esplanade Street and you don't understand why a woman has to have her pigeon-house, but New Orleans is a homecoming, of sorts, for both of us. Diverse and conflicted city, you see me in Degas' pastel, *Ballet Corps Member Fixing Her Hair* while I have only ever seen myself wading out into the Gulf of Mexico.

Tennessee Williams' House (1), Hotel Maison de Ville, 722 Toulouse Street, New Orleans, LA.

Crescent city and I'm thinking of your navel; its curved sickle, the shape of the waning moon. It's getting late, heat shimmers up the sidewalk as I follow the ghostly tap of typewriter keys. I have left you at Pat O'Brien's drinking Hurricanes, to stare up at the tiny white dormer on the tiled roof of the Historic New Orleans Collection. The lunar atmosphere heightens the coloured stucco's blush, but a rubbish skip blocks my view of the façade. Once, in post-coital hush, you told me I had arrived like an angel. In the moon's gloom, the alcove holds the half-shadow of what may not be there.

Tennessee Williams' House (2), Avart-Peretti House, 632 ½ St Peter Street, New Orleans, LA.

When I was little, I wanted to live in a red house with white shutters; a house painted scarlet or vermilion, coloured like a red velvet cake. My mother said it sounded like a brothel, so I spent my childhood dreaming about a brothel with an apple tree in the backyard. You take me to the red house where Tennessee Williams watched the Desire streetcar grind its way through the French Quarter. I look beyond the third floor, enclosing the sky in square brackets of thumbs and forefingers; the clouds are framed, before moving on. In the sun-washed space you place an apple in my palm.

St. Charles Streetcar line, St. Charles Ave, New Orleans, LA.

My dreams begin with the words 'one day'; bright scantlings rising like red balloons. 'One day,' I say, 'we'll drink champagne and eat oysters on the beach'; 'one day, we'll travel to Spain.' But, tethered to your pragmatism, my speculations come to grief. You tell me the closest we can get to the Desire streetcar that rolled through the French Quarter is the St. Charles line. So we alight the olive green tram with the red casements. I remind you that Blanche was told to take the Desire streetcar, transfer to the Cemeteries car and get off at Elysian Fields. For a long while, there is nothing but the smallest zephyr between us. 'One day,' I say, 'I shall die of eating an unwashed grape out on the ocean.' You tell me people don't die from eating dirty grapes.

Faulkner House Books, 624 Pirates Alley, New Orleans, LA.

We're on either side of large French doors. You're leaning against the buttermilk façade of the building watching the sky while I'm browsing the cramped bookshelves inside. I can see the edge of your ear, your elbow and your right shoe's untied lace. I imagine you're looking down the walkway, thinking about Pierre Lafitte's escape from the Calaboose. On our first date you told me you needed space: an uninterrupted view of 'wanton stars and blue meadows'. So I slept on the very edge of your bed and left before sunrise. I move to the side hallway to choose a book of poetry from the two small armoires. I like the nook where my head rests just beneath your collarbone; the gap between your spectacles' bridge and your nose. I think of Faulkner in this front part of his house and imagine he liked to watch the moon descend across Jackson Square.

Carousel Bar, Hotel Monteleone, 214 Royal St, New Orleans, LA.

For three hours we chase Tennessee Williams' shadow around the bar. It takes fifteen minutes for the twenty-five stools to complete a full rotation and nine Mint Juleps for me to hear the quop of his haunted heart beneath the carousing. As you ask the barman questions about the days when Hemingway, Faulkner, Williams and Capote drank here, I imagine the paintings of lions and tigers on the chair backs transforming into footless birds, and snakes that have newly shed their skin. When you're all talked out, you place your hand on my thigh and my heat fogs up the trail of silver cups. I think about asking if you love me, but decide that your answer would be no answer at all.

The Columns Hotel, 3811 St Charles Ave, New Orleans, LA.

You curl my hair slowly, the hot iron occasionally catching my neck. When I pull away, you put your hand on my shoulder and press me back into the chair. My white *Pretty Baby* dress is laid out on the bed next to your digital camera and wallet. You help me into it, stretching the neck to get it over my red lipstick and warm curls. On the way down to the Victorian Lounge I pose on the grand staircase, a bright white speck in your aperture. The green floral wallpaper leans in as you call out, 'I love you once, I love you twice'. You look up at me hopefully, but I can never be Violet to your Bellocq. You like playing cards on rainy days and I can't endure unhappy endings.

Oak Alley Plantation, 3645 LA-18, Vacherie, LA.

I buy pralines at the *New Orleans School of Cooking* for the long bus ride and tuck them into the side pocket of my bag. I'd share them, but you disapprove of me eating sweets before noon. You once told me I mainline sugar; that there are gummy bears and pixie sticks coursing through my veins. And I thought how wonderful that would be. When the tour guide tells us *Oak Alley* was an antebellum sugarcane plantation, you whisper 'sugar baby' in my ear and spend the rest of the ride speed-reading *Interview with the Vampire* over my shoulder. When we disembark, you stand at the top of the allé of double row oak trees and slowly lean me back over your arm. The canopy of leaves makes the clouds look closer. I point at low flying strati and you tell me they are vapour off the Mississippi.

Acme Oyster House, 724 Iberville St, New Orleans, LA.

The glow of neon light brightens our chequerboard table; my face and arms are sunburnt pink. I'm a chess piece waiting for your next move. The waiter hands you an Abita Amber and you call me your checkmate; it's a joke that once would have made me laugh. At the southeast end of the bar you stand me in front of the sign 'Poet's Corner', camera in one hand, beer in the other. I forget to smile. It's little more than a nook for inebriated writers; a fluorescent blue homage to Westminster Abbey. As I'm served a plate of raw Gulf oysters you tell me you've saved me a trip to London.

Second Lining, Decatur St, New Orleans, LA.

Your 'Wild Man Blues' curl like a jellyroll down Decatur, while we march parallel to the Mississippi. No saints come marching in so I hold my umbrella high. Fleur de lys chasing feather boa between the buck-jumping. We're a long way from Earthquake McGoons and those early pre-Crescent days. But you won't play Dixieland now, for anyone. I came here for Tennessee Williams, William Faulkner and the staircase from *Pretty Baby* in the Columns Hotel. You came for the tribute to Bechet at Preservation Hall, its façade like a watercolour or chalk drawing left in the rain. You join the head of the parade, clarinet resting on your curled lower lip, but I stay in the second line, thinking of the Lee Friedlander photograph: *Young Tuxedo Brass Band*, 1966, the old men playing a funeral.

Tremé, Claiborne Ave, New Orleans, LA.

You survived the flooding of the Lower Ninth Ward by taking cover in the bottom quadrant of my heart. Body count zero, I scrawled, to let people know you were safe. I'm your search squad, your protection against natural hazards, your libertarian. Next time the floodwall fails, you'll be waiting for me to save you from the wall of water. There will be room for you, for the seats pulled from the Louisiana Superdome, for mud-caked teddy bears, and even Fats Domino's flood-ruined baby grand piano. I collect brokenness in my left atrium. *Nature repairs her ravages—but not all.*

St. Louis Cemetery, No. 1, Basin at St. Louis St. New Orleans, LA.

In the Cities of the Dead, on the outskirts of the Vieux Carré, you squeeze my hand. I'm imagining being entombed, sealed in one of these above-ground vaults. We cannot return to the earth in a place below sea level, we'll drown. Here, the sun-bleached tombs hold long chambers and the dead are placed on the top shelves, turning to dust and bones in sub-tropical heat. I can't imagine being separated from you for a year and a day, placed in a holding tomb while we slowly bake in individual ovens. You reassure me that in the end, our bones and dust will share the same bag, tucked into the floor of our tomb. I see watermarks like fault lines from the floods on the vaults and imagine coffins set adrift by hurricanes. You put your arm around me. *The living heart of us is bound tight with oak and pine.*

ANONYMOUS

Dates unknown

PAUL MUNDEN

UTC +*/-* • **°**'* / **°**'*

Imagine finding one

abandoned, nameless, while hiking through the jungle, the clean lines of civilisation clotted with centuries of vegetative sprawl; the deeper into wilderness you went, the more likely it became. Today it's re-peopled, its ancient precinct extending down the mountain to hotels—and with a bus service second to none. Fresh from the sauna, you hop on, enjoying the swing around every hairpin bend to the top of the world, where immaculate dry-stone walls are roofed by nothing but mist, as if solidity has given up on itself. Steps lead to rituals and occupations long gone. You marvel at the plan—how it survives its own execution, dissolution, popular acclaim.

You wake, as a young boy

runs to your bedroom, bewildered by his dream—and with a burning question: 'Is there a city where the streets are made of water?' You smile, nod. Affirmation is easy: it's in the surge that pulls you towards the Accademia Bridge, the smell of green canals, the lapping bells ... Harder to grasp is how knowledge can be a gift, like the hand of a stranger, instantly a friend; lightning's sudden description of the lagoon. Some days you feel that gentle rock of water underfoot.

The whiskies behind the bar

stretch almost out of town—yet another claiming to be birthplace of the blues, like those that house the same saint's bones. Their tourist information centres are playing the one riff. Zoom out and it's a tribute concert, so many star guitarists jamming on a global stage. One of course shines, with a MadCat Telecaster that will eventually be displayed, perhaps in the famous club where tonight—after a stranger at the bar has befriended you, and you're ushered through guarded backstage doors—you find yourself the only white man in the room.

Is that King Alfred

with a dustbin lid, standing at the end of the Universal High Street? Global brands have ousted the indigenous, like red squirrels erased by grey, but there's just enough authenticity battling on for a heritage award. The jury is adamant but may have been confused—the supermarket lauded for a stock design: Cathedral City Number 4 (with shelves of generic cheese to match). There may have been bribes. The city has become a Dali monster gorging on its own body with a trowel. Choirboys float across the cathedral close in Harry Potter robes.

Here there are no horizons,

only tunnels you try to navigate with a colour-coded map. Its simple topology marks points of escape, but has no interest in space, or feature—the palaces and statued gardens overhead. You glimpse a rat foraging in the filthy trough that holds the rails, running when it hears a rumble that will soon be dragged—by a grinding light and hot suck of air—into a roar. Bodies press on every side. You try to contain the fear that any day now the backpack crushing against you will explode.

Nothing is to scale

or in its rightful place: Eiffel Tower, Statue of Liberty, and Rialto Bridge straddling a fluorescent canal—all plonked in the old meadows; Paleo-Indians and Latter Day Saints ghosting the new suburbs: Enterprise, Paradise, and Winchester dreaming up a lurid cathedral. Cruise ships have anchored as hotels and casinos—shark reef aquarium *de rigeur*. Once you could sit here with free entertainment, leisurely mushroom clouds blooming in the desert. Today you set up stall in the convention centre, armed with software to stack the odds further in favour of the house. When a troupe of Elvises croons by, you think *Hey—let's get married!*

A leaf changes colour,

reminding you of somewhere else you called home ... and the roads make similar circuits back on themselves, like autumnal thoughts: veer to the left, and another small circle forms a rise of trees, with crimson and eastern rosellas, galahs, red rumped parrots and white cockatoos—a whole lexicon of birds; veer right, and a mob of kangaroos stands to attention, facing you off before resuming their graze. Always nervous of cities, you have found one where you can breathe, the city a lung giving oxygen to the eyes—each vista realigning what you know; a replenishment.

You struggle with his accent

but get the gist of his reply. 'It's like City v United, with religion thrown in, politics too. Four miles between the stadiums. In other places they're right next door. And get this—sometimes they share!' You want to know about the football. He shakes his head. 'I could tell you what I think, but what's that worth? Others'll say different, and it'll end in a fight.' You pay the fare with a generous tip, and after the interview, find a random bar for the match. You watch the partisan crowd witness the goal—or rather, what follows: an innocent abroad, clowning his celebration on a Loyalist flute. You hang your head and don't dare move.

The funfair sets up

like a temporary city on the outskirts of another. Those citizens with the outlandish orange hair and creepy mouths ... they ... you ... you have a vague recollection of a time long ago, wandering similar sideshow streets, in part boredom, part terror, asked to take up a gun and pretend every coconut was a head, with a teddy bear the prize ... Times change. Elephant rides have given way to mechanical thrills: vast carnival wheels and all their rollercoasting variants; turbo drops that leave stomachs in the air. There are those who know of the worn cogs in the machinery, but their tongues are tied.

Ice caps weep into the sea

and the tide washes further above the wooden foundations. It's a decoy—the obvious glittering trophy of doom still holding its own—while on the other side of the world, on higher, safer ground, a sudden, massive wall of water rips a city from its bedrocked roots. Or might. Predictions have all been swept away. You analyse risk with your hi-tech equipment and may as well be staring into the entrails of an owl. Capricious as a god, the new punk climate throws fire in your face, and quietly lets loose the latest *mundus subterraneus*—gone so fast that nobody saw, or was left to tell.

NOTES

Sydney, p. 7

60% of the phrases here come from Francis Webb's Sydney-set poems. I am responsible for the redacting and reordering that have been done to every line. My main wish is that these remixes lead you to the mighty UWAP edition of Webb's *Collected Poems*.

Sydney, p. 8

40% of the phrases here come from Francis Webb's Sydney-set poems. I am responsible for the redacting and reordering as above.

Kyoto, p.21

A version of this poem appears in *Cordite Poetry Review*, vol 57.1, March 2017

Singapore, p. 31

This poem responds to the article 'UK TV drama Cold Feet digitally alters Singapore footage deemed too English' appearing on Channel News Asia, April 4th 2017.

Singapore, pp.39-40

The quote in this poem comes from the *Singapore Times* 'My Turf', 16 Feb 2017.

Mumbai, p. 53

This poem arose from a conversation with Shane Strange in a hip Mexican Bar on a cold evening in Canberra, Australia, where I confessed I once flew across the Bay of Bengal to watch Bryan Adams in concert.
　'Are you serious?' he responded. 'He's really daggy.'
　'What's daggy?' I asked.
　'Uncool,' he said. 'Sort of a has-been. Old, you know?'

Haifa, p. 69

'B.E' is an abbreviation for 'Baha'i Era'—a calendar used in the Baha'i faith.

BIOGRAPHIES

SYDNEY *'I arrived as a 25-year-old. Because of the beauty, I took less than twenty seconds to pledge fealty in perpetuity. Then I took more than twenty years to understand the corruption, but by that time the beauty was an addiction.'*

Ross Gibson tries to live inside this Venn Diagram: New Modes of Writing + New Modes of Heritage Interpretation + New Modes of Art Installation. He is a professor the University of Canberra.

KYOTO *'As a young woman, my wife visted Kyoto on a day trip from Osaka. While sitting in a temple, whose name she can no longer recall, it snowed lightly. "It was like a vision," she said.'*

Shane Strange's writing has appeared in various print and online journals, including *Overland, Griffith Review, Burley, Verity La, foam:e, Cordite Poetry Review,* and *Axon: Creative Explorations.* He is currently studying at the University of Canberra, where he also tutors and lectures in Creative Writing.

SINGAPORE *'I saw this project as an opportunity to interrogate ideas about place and their interplay with plural, intersecting histories, both personal and public. It made sense to focus on the city where I was born, raised and still live. Singapore is still often glossed in reductive terms, but I wanted to make poems that sound out its diverse and often complex landscapes, textures, contours, memories and resonances ... also, Shane made me do it.'*

Alvin Pang is a poet, writer, editor and translator based in Singapore, but active in literary practice worldwide. Among his many engagements, he is a member of the IPSI Advisory Board. Author of over a dozen books, his poetry has been translated into more than twenty languages.

MUMBAI *'My family history links to Mumbai four generations down, and much like Singapore, it is also a kind of home.'*

Pooja Nansi is the author of two collections of poetry, *Stiletto Scars* and *Love is an Empty Barstool*. Her most recent work is her one woman show, *You Are Here* which explores stories of migration and family histories. She teaches Creative Writing at Nanyang Technological University and is also Singapore's inaugural Youth Poet Ambassador.

MOSCOW *'I was born in a small town in Punjab (India). Between 1969 and 1978 I spent nine years in Moscow studying geology. I have lived and worked in many cities, but like Calvino's Marco Polo, every time I describe a city, I seem to say something about Moscow.'*

Subhash Jaireth has published poetry, fiction and nonfiction in English, Hindi and Russian. His short-story collection *Moments* came out in October 2015. His latest book of poetic prose pieces *Incantations* (RWP) was published in September 2016.

HAIFA *'I have had the opportunity to experience the city of Haifa and its surrounds whilst on Baha'i pilgrimage and as a visitor to the Baha'i World Centre. I saw this project as an invitation to contemplate Haifa's unique position, both geographically and historically, and to reflect on the environmental, cultural, and spiritual layers that make up the modern city.'*

Niloofar Fanaiyan is a poet and academic. She has a PhD in creative writing from the University of Canberra and was the 2016 Donald Horne Fellow at the Centre for Creative and Cultural Research. She received the 2016 Canberra Critics Circle Literary Award for Poetry for her book of poems titled *Transit* (RWP, 2016).

CAPE TOWN *'Cape Town is my home town: born there, I spent much of my childhood and adolescence in the city. I left South Africa in the mid-1970s, sailing out of Cape Town and watching it slowly shrink and fade; and didn't return until a few years ago, to find it remarkably the same, startlingly changed.'*

Jen Webb is a poet who researches creativity and cultural practices at the University of Canberra. Her poems have been published in local and international journals and anthologies; she has also published six pamphlet collections, and is editor for the *Australian Book Review*'s 'States of Poetry' annual anthology.

ROME *'Rome is almost imponderable in its historical and cultural richness. While spending six months there on a residency I could not resist writing about aspects of the city that touched my life. These poems are a selection from those works.'*

Paul Hetherington has published eleven full-length collections of poetry, most recently *Burnt Umber* (UWAP, 2016) and *Gallery of Antique Art* (RWP, 2016). He won the 2014 Western Australian Premier's Book Awards (poetry) and undertook an Australia Council for the Arts Literature Board Residency at the BR Whiting Studio in Rome in 2015-16. He is Professor of Writing and head of the International Poetry Studies Institute at the University of Canberra.

NEW ORLEANS *'I've always been obsessed with Dixieland or hot jazz and Oysters Rockefeller. When I was awarded a $15,000 grant for being Deakin University Teacher of the Year, I used the money to go to New Orleans to research hurricane boxes and ate oysters, listening to live jazz in the evenings.'*

Cassandra Atherton was a Harvard Visiting Scholar in English in 2016. She is the successful recipient of more than 15 national and international grants and teaching awards, most recently a VicArts grant and an Australian Council grant for her work on atomic bomb poetry. Her most recent books of prose poetry are *Trace* (Finlay Lloyd) and *Exhumed* (Grand Parade).

ANONYMOUS *'Rather than choosing a single city, I have written about several: all are anonymous, though some will be recognised. With some I have a close connection; others are imaginary, archetypes, or amalgams.'*

Paul Munden is Postdoctoral Research Fellow at the University of Canberra, also Director of the UK's National Association of Writers in Education. His most recent book of poems is *The Bulmer Murder* (RWP) and a further collection, *Fugue,* will be published by UWAP in October.

2016 Editions

Pulse Prose Poetry Project
Incantations Subhash Jaireth
Transit Niloofar Fanaiyan
Gallery of Antique Art Paul Hetherington
Sentences from the Archive Jen Webb
River's Edge Owen Bullock

2017 Editions

A Song, the World to Come Miranda Lello
Cities: Ten Poets, Ten Cities Various
The Bulmer Murder Paul Munden
Dew and Broken Glass Penny Drysdale
Members Only Melinda Smith and Caren Florance
the future, un-imagine Angela Gardner and Caren Florance
Proof Maggie Shapley
Black Tulips Moya Pacey
Soap Charlotte Guest
Isolator Monica Carroll
Ikaros Paul Hetherington
Work & Play Owen Bullock

all titles available from
www.recentworkpress.com

www.ingramcontent.com/pod-product-compliance
Lightning Source LLC
Chambersburg PA
CBHW020617300426
44113CB00007B/675